Praise for Dr. Sevin and
A Beautiful Spiral

"*A Beautiful Spiral* is an incredible testament to the idea that love is the only engine of survival. In this masterful self-exploration, Dr. Ashanna Sevin takes the reader on a journey of her early adulthood, one that involves a near fatal medical illness, a medically induced psychosis, and a brutal violent assault. Through it all, she resists living in a body of fear and, instead, grounds her perceptions and experience within the universal spiritual principles of faith, compassion and forgiveness. She gives the reader a clear example of how these principles can lead one to a higher, more spacious ground, no matter how dire the situation. The book is a must-read for anyone inspired to transform their own traumas, however great or small, into meaningful experiences that further one's journey in a positive manner."

~Jeremy Coles, PhD
Clinical and Forensic Psychologist

"I stood by in the courtroom and witnessed as Ashanna Sevin spoke directly to her assailant. Her powerful declaration to choose love was absolutely riveting and infinitely humbling. This book is a testament to the power and resilience of the human spirit. This story gives a glimpse into what is possible for humanity when we choose compassion in the face of fear. When the pain of life blossoms into healing and love becomes unstoppable."

~Jesse Morris, DC
Doctor of Chiropractic

"Dr. Ashanna Sevin incorporates the rigor of a brilliant mind, the beauty of art, the wisdom of reflection and years of lived experience in her pioneering book, *A Beautiful Spiral.* The wealth of ideas and wisdom presented in this illuminating text will be of benefit to many. This work has the power to transform individual and collective lives."

~Shauna L. Shapiro, PhD
Associate Professor, Santa Clara University,
Co-author of *The Art and Science of Mindfulness*

"Dr. Ashanna Sevin is a powerful, clear-headed woman with a huge smile and a heart of gold, and she carried the burden of her significant health problems with dignity and grace. This is a compelling first-person account of an extraordinary young woman's journey from sickness to recovery, trauma to triumph, loss to redemption."

~John A. Martin, PhD
Licensed Psychologist

"This book is a testament to the fire of the human spirit. In a journey not dissimilar to my own, Ashanna Sevin follows each path that may lead her to a true life of the Spirit. She weaves her illness, pain and trauma into a metaphor that takes her, each time, to a new and deeper level of spirituality, where eventually love and forgiveness win over all. This is the place of inner peace Ashanna had been seeking all through her turbulent life. Her final words are her triumph. As I too have written my memoir with the aid of Elisha Norrie as editor, I can also attest to the surprising insight and further healing that writing one's painful experience can facilitate."

~Denise A. N. Wallis, PhD
Senior Clinical Psychologist, Australia

"*A Beautiful Spiral* is a captivating memoir that leads you through Dr. Sevin's around-the-world travels and deep soul journeys via near-death tragedies and heartwarming celebrations of life. Written from the heart of a person who has experienced hopelessness and demoralization, this piece shows how Dr. Sevin's personal triumph with disease has led her to become a doctor who embodies empathy, gratitude, spirituality and love."

~Mikiko Murakami, DO
Physician of Physical Medicine and Rehabilitation, Mount Sinai Hospital

"A raw and harrowing account of a journey to a place where it literally hurts to be embodied, *A Beautiful Spiral* exhibits a resilience in the face of suffering that is breathtaking. It also traces the compassionate bond between two women, as author and editor, as they share the healing process of restoring the shattered self through words."

~Tracey Slaughter, PhD
Writer and lecturer, University of Waikato, New Zealand

"*A Beautiful Spiral* is not just the story of one individual's path of healing in the face of extraordinary challenges. This book is also a mirror, a story of humanity and our quest for union with the deepest parts of ourselves as we are swept along life's currents – the dark, murky depths and the calm shallows of our lives. This story will humble you. This story will strengthen you. This story will outrage you. But more than that, it will call you into your own heart, where we can choose to stand in the light of our own awareness."

~Laura Larriva Page
Writer, International Performer and Teacher

A Beautiful Spiral

A true story of a healer's journey

DR. ASHANNA SEVIN

A Beautiful Spiral
Written by Dr. Ashanna Sevin
www.abeautifulspiral.com

Edited by Elisha Norrie
www.ElishaNorrie.com

Book jacket design by José Guillermo Sevin

All the names in this book have been changed with the exception of
José Rodríguez, my editor Elisha Norrie,
and my brother Travis.

ISBN-13: 979-8862212136

This book is dedicated to you.
You helped me through my healing journey
When I did not have the strength to keep going
If I was on my own.

Thank you.

Part One

Chapter 1

The Awakening

Blind.

In an instant I was blind.

I was swimming in picture-perfect waters off a beach in Thailand, a welcomed contrast to the parched savannas of northern Namibia. I had just finished serving in the United States Peace Corps and was on my way back to the U.S. to begin my training as a doctor.

A clear view of my life direction had always been important to me even as a child. Going to Africa to serve as a schoolteacher was one of many conscious decisions on my journey to discover who I was and what meaningful purpose my life may have. After spending over two years in the Namibian desert immersed in intense soul-searching and praying for a vision, I finally received clarity: my purpose in life was to be a healer.

So there I was in Thailand. My contract now finished with the Peace Corps, I was enjoying the pleasures of my new freedom knowing that an intense educational journey was about to begin. I was excited, and I was ready. The path ahead was clear. My future was bright.

And then I went blind. And the life I thought I was about to live changed.

Forever.

The water temperature was perfect; warm enough to feel comforting yet cool enough to be refreshing. The beach was not accessible by road so the only way visitors and supplies were shuttled in to this secluded paradise was by aid of the many old boats with flaky paint in muted colors lined up along the shore. And this was my playground. I jumped right into the ocean the first day and began to swim. Although I grew up playing in the water from an early age I was new to freestyle swimming for exercise and so I was concentrating intently on the rhythm of my strokes and breath.

Then all of a sudden my ears filled with pressure and rang with a strange sound. My face was underwater and my eyes were closed when suddenly I could tell something was terribly wrong. I stood up in the chest-deep water and opened my eyes. I expected to see turquoise water bordering white sand with giant limestone rock faces exploding right out of the sea. But I couldn't see any of that in front of me. A huge veil of blackness hung before my eyes. I put my hands out in front of me and waved them around but I couldn't see them at all. The only sight I had was in the far periphery of my visual field that permitted just enough vague light so that I could navigate my way back to shore. Barely. I walked back to the sand with my head turned sideways using this tiny slit of vision.

I sat down. I told myself not to panic. I waited.

What do I do?

My breath quickened. I was terrified. I tried to calm down and force my breath to become slower. I have no idea how long it was, but the blackness began to get smaller. Fainter. My sight slowly returned with every heartbeat, rhythmically coming back in waves.

Finally my normal vision returned. I was in shock and very confused. I felt queasy, ungrounded and very anxious. Then a wave of exhaustion came over me. I just wanted to lie down. I made my way slowly back through the trails in the jungle to my treetop room and slept for a very long time.

I woke the next day and tried to decide what to do. I didn't know what had happened to me the day before. It was terrifying but I didn't know where to go to get it checked out in this tiny beach town that had no hospital or even a doctor's office. The only residents worked at the few hotels or restaurants on that secluded stretch of sand. I surely didn't want to leave this paradise if I didn't need to. And I felt fine that morning. I hoped that it was just a fluke. And not knowing what else to do I decided to continue my vacation as planned and "see" what would happen.

I had already signed up for a three-day rock-climbing package and it was supposed to start that day. Without knowing what else to do I made my way to the little hut where the group was meeting and followed our rock-climbing guide into the jungle. He led us up a winding path into the mountains that led into a cave system. I quickly became absorbed in the beauty around me, and gradually the scare of the day before was left behind. We used head lamps to climb, crawl and squeeze our way through tunnels filled with stalactites and stalagmites until we reached a hole in the rock-face allowing ribbons of sunshine into the darkness. We approached the hole and realized that we were very far from the ground. I volunteered to be the first one belayed down to the bottom and when I landed I met three people who were climbing the rock face below. Little did I know how instrumental these people would be in my life during the following months.

After quick introductions and a friendly chat they invited me to join them for dinner that evening. As we dined outdoors I learned that they lived a few minutes away from my little brother in Denver, Colorado. They were all doctors. The couple was married and the single man was their long-time friend. I was elated to be able to ask some doctors about the episode of blindness, yet they could only offer guesses and theories based on my description. More testing was needed for them to know for sure but they said it might have been a severe electrolyte imbalance and this possibility significantly calmed my fears.

The following day I went out with my rock climbing group again. We were on a multi-pitch climb and I was the lead climber on the second pitch. It was a challenging climb for me. I was shaking with muscle fatigue mixed with the fear of being so far from the ground. I was looking up for a hand-hold and suddenly a black curtain fell before my eyes again.

And I fell.

My last clip attaching the rope to the rock wall wasn't far below me. I had a good partner belaying me who held me tight so I didn't fall very far or hurt myself too badly, but I had to be let down while I hung in my harness – blind. After reaching the ledge I sat on the rock and tried to calm my breathing. Again, after some time that felt like hours, the blackness subsided and slowly disappeared once again to the rhythm of my heartbeat. Again I was left exhausted, so I left the group and carefully made my way back home to sleep.

I told the doctors about what had happened and they could only conclude that I needed further testing to really know what was happening. They could see I was terrified and, even though they didn't know what was going on, they tried to soothe my anxiety and calm me down. They were such a support, and to have an American doctor's attention and advice greatly helped settle my fears.

The doctors were a source of peace over the next few days and we became good friends. And the blindness did not return. By the time we were all leaving the beautiful beach they invited me to come live with them in Denver if I needed a place to stay. They knew I had just finished serving in the Peace Corps and wanted to offer what they could to help me get back on my feet. They had a basement apartment that would be empty by the time I was going to move there and I gratefully accepted.

I didn't have another period of blindness but I was careful, anticipating its return all the time. I left the beach town and took a train to Bangkok to stay with the Thai family of my ex-boyfriend, the man I dated until I entered the Peace Corps. He was half-Thai, half-American and his Thai extended family had a large home and compound in Bangkok. They didn't speak much English except for one cousin and an uncle, yet they all welcomed me with open arms. I was given a guesthouse complete with a baby grand piano and a library filled with beautiful Thai books that I couldn't read. I awoke each morning with the maid knocking on my door saying, "Brek-fast!" in a cheerful Thai accent.

I enrolled in an intense Thai Massage training held at a medical school inside a beautiful temple in downtown Bangkok. Each day I spent studying this ancient art from an old woman who explained more with her hands than with her broken English, and I ravenously absorbed the information and technique. She was tiny, but gave a mean massage and was strong as an ox. If I placed my hands in the wrong place, she would scowl at me and move my hands to the right spot and say, "Yes! Yes! One, two, three! Yes!" I never really figured out what the "one, two, three" was referring to, but she was a stickler for details, and she made sure I got it right. Or else…

After a few weeks of the maid's "brekfasts" and the Thai masseuse's strict lessons, I began to experience some intense pain deep in my abdomen. I could feel something hard and extremely painful inside me that made it nearly impossible to sit down at times. The uncle of the family happened to be one of the head honchos at the top hospital in the country. I told him about the pain one morning over "brekfast" and he took me to the hospital with him that day, handed me off to some doctors and assured me that I was in good hands.

They did some tests and then told me I had a cyst in my lower abdomen, an infection of some sort, and that I would need minor surgery. They put me in a gown and rolled me into a poorly lit, dirty room and began to put needles in my skin near the source of the pain, little shots with anesthetic that I swear to God did not work at all. I was totally awake and terrified. Then they took a scalpel and cut through my skin to reach the cyst inside of me. I screamed and felt my eyes fly open with pain. But it was over before I knew it, and I felt a warm flow of liquid oozing out of the incision. They said I didn't need stitches and that it was best if I left it open to drain, though they did put a bandage over it. The whole procedure was done within about fifteen minutes and then they wheeled me into another room to get dressed. They gave me some sanitary pads to wear and sent me outside to catch a taxi back home. So there I was: a twenty-six year old woman crying on the sidewalk in the middle of Thailand, bleeding, scared, tired and wanting my mama more than I had ever wanted her in my life.

I rested for the next couple of days. I was finished with the Thai Massage course and was in too much pain to walk around the city, so I gazed at the Thai books in the library in my guesthouse and slept a lot. On the third day I took my compact mirror and tried to gaze at the incision. I saw a small nasty-looking black thing protruding out of the cut. I touched it and it didn't hurt. I couldn't figure out what it was so I took my tweezers and began to pull, and pull and pull. A long black slimy thing kept coming and coming out of this hole in my body. I reeled thinking it was a long worm. After watching all those crazy healthcare movies in Namibia I was convinced it was a parasite that was exiting my body. Finally I got to the end of it and I took it to the sink and laid it down. After a careful inspection it turned out to be a long piece of gauze they had stuffed inside of me without telling me. Lord. At that point I was ready to go home.

My flight back to the States left a couple of days later. I wore a huge sanitary pad on the plane and blood still soaked through to the seat from sitting so long on the incision. I flew to Atlanta first to see my parents and was so excited to be home with family and surrounded by familiar things. I rested, showed photographs and just soaked up their presence, as it had been years since I had seen some of them. The wound from the surgery in Thailand appeared to heal nicely after a while.

Good, chapter closed.

I applied for school to take my medical prerequisites and was ready to start this exciting new phase of my life: the path to become a healer.

I arrived in Denver in May just before the summer quarter was to start, and went to the doctors' house that I had met in the little beach town in Thailand. I moved into their basement and started classes shortly thereafter. It turned out that the amount of hours I was able to transfer over from my previous degree, plus the hours of prerequisite classes that I now had to take to get into medical school, enabled me to obtain a second degree, so I put together an individualized degree called "Health Science Foundations". I began taking anatomy, statistics, abnormal psychology, microbiology, and the like. I also landed a wonderful job on campus as a personal trainer working with people with physical disabilities. I began to get to know the students that I worked with and a general sense of happiness and well-being came over me.

I had just returned from fulfilling a long-time dream of mine to travel the world and had spent over two years in service in Namibia with people I loved dearly. Through that experience and my travels afterwards, I had been exposed to many cultures and beliefs that had blown my small-town-Georgia world right apart, in a good way. I really felt I had grown so much as a person and now I was on my way to fulfill my calling to become a doctor, to continue serving others and have a settled career. I found myself smiling a lot.

It was the beginning of summer and the weather was beautiful, so I started jogging down the tree-lined streets of Denver in the early evenings. The air was crisp and invigorating, and the runs became my favorite part of the day. But suddenly I started experiencing strange sensations that I could not explain, that came over me during the jogs. It felt like my brain went a little tingly, a little fuzzy. I noticed that it only happened when I was exercising. These "strange periods," I started calling them, didn't last too long, especially if I stopped running and just walked a bit. But the "strange periods" always left me feeling a bit tired. I did not go blind again, thank God, but my reality altered just a little. Everything looked as if I had put on those soft plastic glasses that make everything look like it has a rainbow halo around it. My head tingled and I had a small pressure in my ears. The world just felt strange for these short periods of time.

Again, I spoke with the doctors about it at home and they were only left guessing, and I was just too scared to have it checked out more thoroughly. Not to mention I didn't have health insurance. I had only been back in the States for a few weeks and had very little money so I hadn't dealt with the issue of insurance yet. Also, the episodes always went away and didn't seem too threatening. I think I was in denial that anything was really wrong, hoping that if I ignored it, it would all just go away.

Then one day I was in the student gym taking an aerobics class. We were in the middle of an intense aerobics section when suddenly a wonderful feeling washed over me, the most intense and pleasurable thing I could ever remember feeling. It was ecstatic!

I had exercised a lot in my lifetime and I was familiar with runner's high but this was clearly more than that. It crossed my mind that maybe I should stop doing the aerobics. I thought it was some sort of crazy runner's high that was out of control and if I stopped it might go away. But it just felt so damned good so I decided to keep going and ride it out. I could not believe the incredible carnal sensations I felt. Then I had visions come to me of different landscapes. The first one was mountainous and I knew that somehow it represented my mother and I was filled with love. My whole heart filled with more love than I had ever experienced from my mother, towards my mother. And then another landscape flashed before me, this time what looked like the Grand Canyon with an eagle flying overhead, and this was my brother Travis. I was again washed with ecstatic love that filled every inch of me.

That was the last thing I remember.

I was told later that after we had finished the aerobics session and cooled down we made our way down onto the floor and started doing an abdominal workout. I don't remember any of that. But sometime in the middle of doing sit-ups I started having a grand mal seizure. The staff of the athletic center had become my friends by that point and they were terrified by what they saw and immediately called 9-1-1. There happened to be a fireman they knew in the building and someone ran to get him.

He arrived while I was still seizing and made sure I was safe and calmed people down. Apparently I was seizing hard. For a long time.

The first thing I remember after the ecstatic vision of the Grand Canyon was the ambulance staff trying to get me to stand up and walk. "Just get up and walk. You must try to walk. Here, we will help you," as they tried to help me up and move me forward. It was as if I was looking through a foggy tunnel. I could barely understand their words and I could not walk. My legs were completely limp like jelly and I was groggy as hell. I don't remember getting on a gurney or getting into the ambulance. I only remember waking up in the hospital to a doctor at my bedside.

"Ma'am, I am Dr. Johnson. You are in the hospital right now. We found that you have six brain tumors. Are you aware that those tumors are there?"

"No…," I stammered, confused and bewildered. Was this real? Was I dreaming? Was I dead? I began to falter. I thought about what had just happened to me. My memory was muddled but I recalled being in the aerobics class, the visions and the ecstatic blissful feeling I felt in my body before the ambulance arrived.

Dr. Johnson explained to me that sometimes people were brought into the hospital and already knew they had brain tumors. He had to ask me just in case. Since we didn't know what they were, they needed to do some tests to figure out what type of growths were in my brain. "Just relax. We will take care of you the best we can," he promised. "A nurse will be by shortly. Rest now."

After a few hours of interrupted sleep, a few of my friends from the athletic complex came in to visit me. Keisha, an amazing basketball player, had a way with words and she was able to put me more at ease. She joked with me and told me how much I had freaked them all out with the seizure, how they had called 9-1-1 and found the fireman upstairs. She somehow got me to laugh at how they handled the situation. She was such an animated, sweet young woman and I was so glad to have her company.

I stayed in the hospital for quite awhile. How long? I could not tell. The doctors did every test under the sun to try to find out what the tumors were. I felt like I was being poked and prodded all day long. I don't know why they needed to take my blood so many times but it gave me the opportunity to become friends with the heavily pierced and tattooed phlebotomist. I had a CAT scan, an MRI, a spinal tap and x-rays, yet every test they did came back negative. I was finally told that it was probably cancer, tuberculosis or some other terrible disease that I can't even remember the name of now. They told me they were going to test for everything else first and only do a biopsy for cancer as a last resort, as that involved drilling through my skull and inserting a needle into one of the tumors to extract a piece of it to test.

One by one the lab tests came back negative. It wasn't tuberculosis either. I laid in the hospital bed and it seemed like I was in the eye of a storm. Somehow I felt like I was the only peaceful one. My family, understandably, was extremely upset and worried. The doctors and nurses, oh so many of them, swarmed around me in a flurry of confusion as the tests continued to tell them nothing.

Finally, a doctor told me that all the latest tests were negative and everything was pointing towards cancer. He said there was still one lab test they were waiting for from the Center for Disease Control and Prevention in Atlanta. It was a test for a strange infectious disease but the tech at the CDC told them that it would probably be negative. He said he had tested hundreds of returned Peace Corps Volunteers for this disease and not once had anyone tested positive. But, considering my travel history, they had to try it. After those results came back, they would know for sure if it was negative and then they would take me in for a biopsy. The biopsy was scheduled for later that day. He was just trying to tell me the facts so I could prepare myself.

During that long time alone in my room, I began to take stock of my life. I looked up at the ceiling and thought to myself, "Well, this could be it. I could die soon." And somehow, amazingly, I felt OK with that.

I was twenty-six years old. I had just come back from traveling all over the world and had experienced the adventure of a lifetime. I had known true love and friendship and had followed a deep spiritual path. In many ways I felt fulfilled. Perhaps I was stunned into a place of emptiness, but it felt like peace. Sweet, easy peace. All the worries I had had the week before about homework and exams and bills were all so irrelevant now. There was nothing to worry about. Nothing worth stressing over. When you get jerked backwards so fast and hard, you gain a different perspective and the things you normally stress over seem absolutely meaningless.

This time while waiting to find out what kind of brain tumors I had and if I was going to live or die prompted me to also look back over my life. It felt important to take this opportunity, perhaps the last opportunity, to really look at my life. I needed to quietly witness myself, celebrate my journey and how I had evolved over the years to become the woman I was now – and may not be for much longer.

Chapter 2

Georgia Peach

I was playing in the front yard of our house in a small town in Georgia when my sweet Grandma Jane told me that my mom was coming home from the hospital. I didn't understand why she was gone but I was excited she was coming home. I picked some flowers for her; actually they were weeds, a small token of love from a child that knew no other world. My mom got out of the car in her cream-colored nightgown and walked very slowly. The sun shone brightly in the chilly air and her waist length blonde hair caught every single ray that was offered, shining like golden silk threads. She was so beautiful.

She was holding him. Travis. She brought him into the house and put him on the bed. I was given a small light-blue hairbrush, the kind where the bristles are so soft it almost feels like hair itself. I was not yet three and was barely tall enough to see him on the bed, but I timidly walked up to him and just looked at him with the wide-eyed awe that only a child can have. I was told to be gentle with him. I reached out and touched him, smelled him. And brushed his hair. For a long, long time.

When I was little I would wear my dad's work boots that came up to my upper thighs. I wore tons of big beaded necklaces and rings all over my tiny fingers from my mom's jewelry box and walked around the house like I was a queen. A queen that wore thigh-high boots of course. And danced. I loved to dance. My favorite thing was to have a dance party on top of the pool table with my little brother. I didn't seem to understand that he needed a diaper on if he was going to dance up there with me…

When I was four years old, I was bouncing a ball and playing in the waiting room of my big brother's orthodontist. All of a sudden the ball got out of my control and bounced away, rolling across the room. A large African American woman picked up the ball and walked up to me holding out her hand with the ball in her palm. I was scared of her, as I was typically shy and she was so big, but I mustered the courage to reach out and take my ball. My mom looked at me and said, "Now, honey, what do you say?" expecting me to say a big "thank you" to the stranger. Yet instead, I said in my shy little four-year-old voice, "I don't talk to black people."

My mom has retold this story to me, and how a flood of embarrassment washed over her as she stammered to the woman, "I am so sorry, ma'am. I have not taught her that. I am not sure why she said that." The woman mumbled that it was OK and moved on. I definitely did not learn that from my open-minded, loving family. I must have learned that response from one of my friend's parents.

My small-town Georgia neighborhood was racially mixed, about half African American and half white. There was also a full spectrum of prejudiced people including some whites, who strangely enough, would go to church and preach about how much God loved everyone yet in the same breath would curse the African Americans and call them terrible names. Then there were those who were in interracial relationships and were strong enough to stand up for open acceptance despite the names they were called by their neighbors. Most people were pretty outwardly indifferent yet still held some sort of racial hierarchy in their minds.

I am still not sure which household I learned that I should not talk to African Americans, but my mama was right, it was not from ours. But as

I grew up with heated racial tension at school there were unwritten rules when it came to race. At high school, a white girl who dated an African American guy was socially labeled by most of my peers, and most of the white guys that I knew would never ask her out after that.

Once when I was a freshman, a gorgeous African American senior athlete called me up and asked me out. I declined, saying that I found him to be wonderful, but I was not ready to give up being asked out by white guys over it, and I hoped he understood. He muttered that he did, and I hung up the phone feeling good, as if I had just spoken my truth from my heart. Plain and simple. To this day I cringe when I think about that conversation, and although there are not many things I wish I could take back in my life, I wish I could eat my own words from that day and apologize to that young man. I have since dated and been in love with men of color from all over the world, and it still blows my mind that I was so steeped in those racial labels from Georgia in the 1980s that I did not know any better than to say something like that. But I did.

We played together all the time, Travis and me. Almost three years apart but of like mind, we rode our bikes around, played Nerf football, built forts out of sheets, put together seemingly miles of racecar tracks through our house, complete with loops and turns, and built cities out of Legos. We even slept in the same room for years, as I preferred to be in a sleeping bag on his floor rather than sleep in my own room. We never really fought – except once. We were both taking tae kwon do. I was eleven and Trav was eight. He was a green belt and I was a yellow belt. I remember it well. I had my first crush in that martial arts class – an all consuming, butterflies-in-the-tummy kind of crush. Sadly, it was also my first experience of unrequited love.

One day Travis and I started wrestling, a normal activity for us so we actually were quite organized. There was an imaginary boxing ring that conveniently fit inside our family room. We stood on opposite corners and took turns ringing the bell that started the round. We somehow were careful to try our best to pin the other to the floor without hurting one another. Until tae kwon do came along, and one day it got a little out of hand. A little pain here, some frustration there and before you knew it we were full-on sparring instead of wrestling. And there is a huge difference, my friend.

After a few kicks and punches I thought, "Now Trav is only eight. He hasn't hit puberty yet. If I kick him in the balls, it probably won't hurt that bad." And so I did.

Yeah… That was the end of it: the end of the fight, and the end of him breathing – for quite a long moment – if I remember correctly. That was the last time we fought, and the last time we even wrestled. Just in case.

I do not recall talking about spirit or God in our house when I was growing up. I had no words to put to the feelings I had inside of me. But my spirit burned inside me, tugging at me. A part of me as real as any other part; be it arm or leg or heart. When I was in my first year of high school some friends invited me to go to church with them. We were good friends so I said yes, not knowing what I was in for. Despite the fact that we had a church on almost every corner in that small Georgia town I had never been to one before.

When I arrived, there was a lot of activity going on. People everywhere. They separated the youth from the children from the adults, and each group went their separate way. The youth were led to a house across the street from the church where we all sat closely on the floor. It was packed. A "revival" was happening. I had no idea what that was at the time but I was interested. The youth minister asked, "Do you feel like you have a hole in your heart and want to fill it and don't know how?" I thought to myself, "Yes. I know exactly what this man is talking about."

And strangely, I knew it wasn't going to be filled by my family or a boy-friend or any amount of success.

I was so aware of my spirit inside of me even though I didn't have the language to talk about it. I had a feeling of incompleteness that no matter how good my days were there was still something missing. "Well," the youth minister said, "The only thing that will ever fill it is Jesus Christ." He started speaking about having a relationship with God. Talking to Him, listening to Him, spending time with Him. Actually having an active relationship with God. He said that God loved me so much, and if I only asked Him, He would come into my heart and fill that hole. Finally reuniting me with Him. He was so passionate, so believable. I was just flabbergasted that someone was speaking so plainly of something I had never spoken of before with anyone. I didn't even know if other people felt that hole in their hearts, in their innermost. At the end of his sermon he asked if anyone wanted to say a prayer with him and ask God to enter their hearts. I did. And so I joined the church, got baptized and went every Sunday. And every Sunday night. Then Wednesday. And eventually door-to-door on Mondays.

The youth group was full of some very special people. There was wonderful support from the adults in the church, too. There were always activities to do and fun trips to go on. I had community, real community. Like-minded people who loved me and included me. I loved that.

My relationship with God also flourished. Truly. I didn't just sit in church; I read my Bible all the time. Highlighting things, understanding things, not understanding things and asking questions about it. I spent time every day in prayer, on my own, with my friends, with my youth group. I constantly asked for forgiveness for my sins, thanked God for everything in my life; I asked for help in areas of my life and for the prayer requests other people had given me. At church I listened intently to the preacher who was a very enthusiastic fire-and-brimstone speaker. I sang the hymns and cried and felt so connected to God sometimes. That hole in my heart was completely filled. Right down to the core. And although it wasn't common in my church, I spoke in tongues sometimes. I just felt that if I let go and didn't let words get in the way I could just speak and God would understand. It was so freeing and so intimate. I would collapse onto my knees and weep at the altar feeling such thanks that God loved me. That He sent His only Son to die for me, this wretch that didn't deserve it, which was the message I was taught. I believed it fully.

This path to God had structure. I thrived with structure. This is how you talk to God, this is what you read to understand God, this is where you go to learn about Him and this is what you say in your prayers. It was solid enough for me to grasp on to and run with it. And there was such community all believing the same thing, doing the same thing. It was comforting that way.

But I was racked with guilt. I truly believed that guilt came from God to show us when we had done something wrong. I said so out loud in church one time, in an open forum in the sanctuary. No one came to correct me. No one said anything. Perhaps they thought it was a good thing, that it kept me being a good girl. Maybe they all thought the same thing. But it ate at me. I would sing that sweet song with conviction: "Amazing grace, how sweet the sound that saved a wretch like me." I was taught that just by being born I was a sinner and I never could deserve what God had done for me by sending His only begotten son to die for me. Even when I wasn't "sinning" I could still try to tell more people about Jesus (oh, their blood was on my hands, all of them, if I didn't tell them). I could still pray more. I was just never enough, which oddly was exactly how I felt around my parents.

I spent my entire high school experience dedicated to the church and my spiritual path. It kept me innocent and inexperienced when it came to things like drugs, parties and sex. And gave me a whole inner world – a deep, incredibly intimate relationship with God that is very difficult to explain.

When I graduated from high school I went on a self-initiated retreat. I took my car up into the mountains and stayed at a huge log cabin that was owned by a couple at my church. I spent a full twenty-four hours fasting and in prayer asking God to help me stay true to Him while I was in college. I knew I was going to be tempted with a whole new life and new influences, and I was dedicated to my walk with God. I didn't want to stray.

I started Georgia Tech in the fall of 1991. My parents had just gotten a divorce and the stress at home was devastating to me, so I relished the new life I began when I went to college. I moved into a dorm on campus and loved it right from the start: the smell of the fall air, the sound of the drum corps practicing throughout the campus, the rite of passage into adulthood with my new freedom, and I cherished the intellectual stimulation. I joined the Baptist Student Union (BSU) and they became my family. We studied together, played together, read the Bible, and prayed together and supported one another.

At this point in my Christian walk I began to have doubts, questions. I truly didn't understand this system of there being a heaven and a hell, and if you asked Jesus to come into your heart with these specific words then you would go to heaven and if you didn't you would go to hell *for eternity*. What about all those people in Africa who have never heard of Jesus' name? Would they burn in hell due to their ignorance? What about a child who isn't old enough to learn about Jesus yet? The clear-cut version of how the afterlife worked just didn't sit right with me. I asked questions to my elders at church and at the BSU. I was told to have faith. "Just have faith, the blind faith of a child." So I continued on my way, struggling to muster the faith that I needed.

During my first year at Georgia Tech I was supposed to decide what I wanted to do for the rest of my life and declare a major. I had no clue as to what my purpose was in life or what kind of job I wanted when I "grew up." For want of any clear sense of "what I wanted to be" I decided to choose what I was most interested in, which was physics. I had a wonderful friend in high school that continually lent me books on physics such as *The Tao of Physics*, *The Dancing Wu-Li Masters*, *Chaos* and others, and I was fascinated by it all. Also, my father was a bit of an astronomy buff and so my parents had sent me to space camp when I was thirteen. I loved black holes, the idea of what was on the other side, and the sheer enormity and mystery of the universe. I was fascinated by the subject, secretly loving that line when science and academic knowledge stopped, and even the most brilliant scientists had to throw up their hands and say, "And the rest is a mystery." I felt like that was where Spirit lived. I really got into quantum mechanics and astrophysics. Somehow when things got so small or so big that we couldn't see it anymore I loved it. I felt like I was exploring the edges of our universe.

During my sophomore year I finished taking all the classes in astrophysics that the university offered. I asked the astronomy professor if there was anything more I could take and expressed my interest in the topic. He listened to the list of classes I had taken and said that there was nothing more for me to enroll in. However, he had a special project in mind that I could work on as an independent study course and I immediately agreed. I liked him immensely both as a teacher and on a personal level and I knew that it would be a great experience.

The first thing we worked on was writing some software to sort the stars that we were working with into appropriate categories so we could map them. He had worked with an astronomer in Michigan that was systematically going through each star in the sky and recording its magnitude and other information into a spectral catalog. It was the first work of its kind in which the same person was ranking each star. We filtered out the stars that had the most reliable data and were able to push the numbers through several equations in order to estimate how far away each star was, therefore mapping the universe. We plotted the stars in Aitoff projection plots that showed the position in a 360-degree view, much like mapping the globe onto a two-dimensional surface. We then calculated how old each star was, separating them into different star types. Through this method, we were able to show which galaxies were babies and which had been around for a long time.

We wrote several articles that were being refereed for journal publication, and applied for and received a grant from the National Science Foundation to take this work to the American Astronomical Society meeting in Washington, DC. It was a fascinating experience. Not only was I able to produce some quality papers worthy of being published in respected scientific journals but was able to attend the American Astronomical Society meeting and check out the work of many physicists from across the country. I also had to present our own work to many of those top physicists. It was an honor and a very humbling yet uplifting experience. And I am pretty sure I was the only nineteen-year-old girl there – complete with permed hair and *very* high bangs.

The following year my roommates came home with a flier announcing the first study abroad program for our university. I immediately wanted to go, even if the subject matter was not in my major. I had never been overseas before and I wanted the experience of living in Europe. It just so happened that they were studying something very cool. They were offering a certificate in Biomedical/Rehabilitation Engineering at Oxford University in England. I applied to the program, got accepted and started taking extra engineering courses that were needed in order to participate in the program.

Once at Oxford the studies were amazingly interesting. We had a project to design a bed for a quadriplegic that would allow the person to go to the toilet in the bed, roll him/her throughout the day so they wouldn't get bed sores, have the option to bathe the person in the bed, plus a lift to get the person into a wheelchair. We spent the quarter researching materials and lifts and even how to prevent bedsores. We had to present our inventions to a board of Oxford professors. I was chosen as the point presenter for the group, as the rest of my team was very shy.

During the program we studied prosthetic limbs, straight from some of the top producers in the world. We saw how they engineered a prosthetic hand to register electrical impulses in the arm where the muscles would have been and have the hand act out what the real hand would have done. I saw how they programmed it to grasp something as light as a feather. And when picking things up, to only close if the object started to slip: gentle enough so as not to break an egg yet firm enough to be able to pick up a hammer. They showed us the fake skin they had designed with the help of Hollywood special effects teams. The prosthetic arm had hair, freckles and wrinkles in the right places. You could hardly tell it was a fake – and it was almost fully functional. Amazing.

During the week we took fascinating field trips all over England, eating cucumber sandwiches and trying to look the part of cool young travelers (at this point my hair had lost the huge bangs. Thank God). I frequently skipped classes to see Shakespearean plays in Stratford-on-Avon and Vivaldi symphonies in gorgeous churches. I loved every minute.

One day I was in deep conversation with some friends in the program and I started telling them about my conversion to Christianity. This was the way I "witnessed," or told people about Christ and tried to convert them, if they wanted to. I had reached a middle ground somehow from my church's teachings. I never felt comfortable telling people as if I were preaching. But I felt good, though nervous and uncomfortable every time about sharing my own experience about my walk with God, and then seeing if the person had any interest after that. These two fellows were practicing Buddhists and happened to be the first Buddhists I had ever spoken to, and they shared their own spiritual beliefs with me too. The conversation, in the end, led to *me* being more interested in Buddhism rather than them being more interested in Christianity.

All those questions I had asked my elders and was told "just have faith" were still pulling at my sleeves. I allowed these questions to have a little more airtime in my thoughts. Some of the things the Buddhists had said made sense too. It was truly my first exposure to a spiritual path other than Christianity. A way to be with God and have that hole in my heart filled with Spirit and yet not be embedded in the Christian dogma. I was confused.

When I returned for my senior year of university I did a bold thing. All my spiritual questions and wonderings had come to a head. So one crisp fall day I sat in prayer. I had never prayed a more earnest prayer in my life. I asked God, begged God for the truth. "All I want to know is the truth," I pleaded. "And if the truth is what I have been believing and following all these years, then wonderful, because all my friends are Christian, all my music is Christian – my whole life is wrapped up in it. But if that is not the truth then I want to know even if it means leaving all that I know."

And so I started at the beginning. Did I believe in God? Why or why not? I thought about it. Felt it. What did I believe and why? What was God like and how can I be close to Spirit? I allowed myself to ask these kinds of questions and answer them slowly – slowly. I had to pull away from all of my friends, ignore their calls and not listen to them when they told me they were praying for me because I was straying from the path.

And my questioning led me down a very different path. One that is still unfolding to this day.

Chapter 3

Cerebral Cysticercosis

I was still reminiscing over my earlier life when a doctor suddenly rushed in and babbled quickly, "The one test that we were told by the CDC that never came back positive? Well, your test results were positive! The tumors you have in your brain are actually worms. You have a condition called Cerebral Cysticercosis. It is a parasite. This is a rare condition to see in the United States."

It was such a shock. Of all the scenarios I had been preparing for I had not even considered this one.

He went on to explain how the parasitic cycle worked; "The mother worm is one of those long intestinal parasites. She grows to be around twelve feet long and can live to be thirty years old. She periodically lays thousands of eggs in the intestines of the person or animal she is living in and these little eggs come out in the stool. If someone goes to the bathroom and gets some of the eggs on their hands and does not wash them off then they can be transmitted to any food they touch. If another person eats the food with the eggs on it then that person becomes infected. The eggs are so small at this stage that they pass through the lining of the small intestine and travel through the body in the blood. They leave the vessels at various places and can lodge into muscles, onto the backs of the eyeballs – or they can go directly into the brain."

"What about the intestinal parasite? Do I have one of those, too?" I asked.

"No," he said, "although we would like to do another stool test to make sure you don't. But we don't think so." He then explained how the intestinal mama worm is transmitted when undercooked pork is eaten. Human feces are often fed to pigs in third-world countries. And if a pig eats the stool of an infected human then thousands of eggs enter the pig's body. The eggs are so small at that point that they travel through the intestinal wall and go to the muscles, brain or eyeballs of the pig and grow into larvae. If a person eats some infected pork that is not cooked all the way then this larva can grow into a long intestinal worm in that person and thus the cycle continues.

Humans are the only known host of the adult worm that grows in the intestines. But if a human has a long worm living in their bellies they might not even know it. Occasionally they might get diarrhea but often times there are no symptoms. The worms operate in a continual cycle that passes from humans to pigs to humans. Once the larvae enter the muscles, eyes or brain they cannot reproduce – it is kind of like a beehive. Only the big queen can have the babies. And the worms in my brain were in the dead-end portion of the parasite's life cycle. Luckily I tested negative for a mama worm living in me.

The doctors explained that I had picked up the parasite while living on my homestead in Namibia. The growths were all different sizes and suggested that I had been continually infected with eggs the entire time I was in Namibia. Some were larger and looked to be two years old and some had more recently entered my system. They theorized that someone in the family I lived with had a mama worm living in their gut. Since the intestinal worms live so long there is no telling how long it had been there. They had probably contracted it from eating pork at someone else's homestead at some point. But the ones I had in my brain were from the eggs that were transmitted by the fecal/oral route from a person infected with the mama parasite in their gut. Without running water it was quite common for someone to defecate in the fields or use the latrine then never wash their hands afterwards. Actually, I never remember seeing them wash their hands, especially with soap, after using the bathroom. And we shared meals together all the time, eating with our hands as a group, out of big baskets of food.

The fact that I contracted the parasite during my Peace Corps service turned out to be a big blessing for me. This meant that the U.S. government was responsible for all of my allopathic medical costs related to this condition, a burden I never would have been able to bear if I was all on my own.

The doctors told me that I probably had many worms living in my muscles. Yet the worms in human muscles don't seem to bother them most of the time. They sent me to an ophthalmologist to see if I had any attached to my eyeballs. I was scared about those because I was told that they have to be surgically removed. It was an uncomfortable procedure for them to check behind my eyeballs, to say the least, but thank God I didn't have any worms back there.

The worms that make it into the brain can cause all sorts of neurological problems. Some I had already experienced: the periods of mysterious blindness while I was in Thailand, the "strange periods" I had when I exercised, which turned out to be a sort of seizure. They were all part of it. The list of possible symptoms is a page long and span from seizures of all magnitudes, to dementia, headaches and death. Actually, I later found out that over 50,000 people a year die from Cerebral Cysticercosis and it is the leading cause of adult-onset epilepsy in the world.

Here's the catch: when the eggs enter the brain they are so small that they don't usually cause a problem at first. They program cells of the host's body to surround it and form a semi-permeable cyst that grows with it during its five to seven year life span. They filter nutrients into the cyst that would normally go the brain, and they defecate, dumping the waste into the brain through the cyst wall when the toxicity inside the cyst becomes too much for them. The worms can grow up to a few centimeters long and thus the cysts have that same diameter. And since the cyst is made out of your own body's material the immune system leaves it alone, not knowing there is a creature inside of it. The worms can grow for years undetected, so many growths cause a major disruption in the electrical circuitry in the brain as well as putting pressure in areas all over the brain. Sometimes this causes glands to over- or under-produce hormones and can cause many other problems.

When one of the worms finally dies, the cyst wall no longer has anything to program it to stay together and it breaks open revealing to the body that a worm is in the brain. A dead worm. The immune system freaks out and attacks it full force, and the sudden and extreme swelling inside the skull can be enough to kill people. I apparently had one that died prematurely and the swelling that occurred is what caused the blindness in Thailand and eventually the grand mal seizure. The doctors said they could tell by the brain scans that one of them had a lot of heat and swelling around it, thus indicating that it had died and my body's immune system was reacting and trying to kill whatever it was and take the foreign material out of the brain. It caused such a disturbance to the brain's electrical activity that I had a seizure. The rest of the worms were all still alive and kicking or squirming or whatever they do – eating and excreting their waste inside my brain – their own personal paradise.

The infectious disease doctor explained that if they were to give me drugs to kill them then all of the cysts might break open at once which would definitely be enough to kill me. So there were other drugs: drugs to suppress the immune system so that there wouldn't be so much swelling in the brain all at once, and drugs to block the seizures, which I had been taking since after the first seizure. There were also other options. There was brain surgery. But the worms were all over my brain so the surgery was going to be very invasive and difficult to perform. Or we could do nothing but try to mask the seizures and other symptoms as they came. Some research suggested that option. But I had to decide. He said I should think about it.

I went home and caught up with my friends and told them the news. The doctors that I lived with immediately called their friend that was with them in Thailand. It turned out that he was an infectious disease doctor, and since this was classified as an infectious disease he was interested in my case. He came over to the house and told me to tell him everything.

He listened to my story intently, aghast and totally fascinated by the news. It turned out that the doctor he worked under was the most respected and knowledgeable doctor in the state of Colorado to deal with that particular condition, but at the time she was not seeing new patients. He spoke with her about me and asked if she would treat me. She agreed. So I transferred my care to her. A blessing! A crazy synchronicity I could hardly believe.

She strongly suggested the drug route over surgery or masking the symptoms, and that was the direction my family and I were leaning toward anyway. I knew that the drug cocktail was experimental but she seemed confident and knowledgeable and I felt it was all meant to be due to the amazing series of events that led me to meet her.

I had to get in touch with the Peace Corps and tell them the news. I wanted to get word to the family I had lived with and any other volunteers that might be in the area in case of other infections. Up in my old village people never really knew what was wrong with them when they got sick. There was a hospital not too far away, the one I used to volunteer in after I finished teaching at the village school each day, but it was always packed with people and difficult to be seen by a doctor. Often they wouldn't have the medication needed, even basics like antibiotics. It was such a shame, and many people died of easily curable illnesses because of the lack of simple medications that are so readily available in other parts of the world.

Also, since most people did not make it to the doctor when they were sick, often nobody knew what illness they had. Therefore the villagers labeled most things as a "headache" even if the person didn't actually have pain in their head at all. People would die and they would regularly say, "Oh, she died of a headache," or "he died of a headache," no matter what the symptoms were. I think that most of the time it was actually AIDS. It was quite rampant in Namibia, but there was no diagnosis or words to match the sickness. So, "it's a headache" became the catchall phrase.

I had never known any of the kids I was living with to have a seizure or anything, but I was worried about them. They might just say it was a headache and not get the help they needed. Then I remembered that there was a man on the Peace Corps staff who used to be a volunteer in that village before I was, so I made a call to him, told him the news and about my concerns. He took word to the village. I never heard anything back. I hoped that no news was good news.

My new doctor explained that patients were usually hospitalized for the entire three weeks during the administration of the medication for Cerebral Cysticercosis. It seemed to have all sorts of possible and terrible side effects and no one knew for sure which ones I would have. But my mother was adamant about staying with me every second and pleaded for us to be able to go home if I was under her care. She promised to take me to the hospital if there was a hint of a serious problem. The doctor finally acquiesced, which I was very thankful for.

I am so thankful to her for being such a great mama. She held her word, and stayed with me 24/7, taking care of me and holding me in love. We watched my body like a hawk but my side effects were mild compared to what some others experienced. But due to the steroids I was taking I broke out in a terrible rash all over my body, gained thirty pounds seemingly overnight, got very moody and generally didn't feel like myself.

Even though I was resting at home, I kept thinking about the Peace Corps and my two years spent in that little village in northern Namibia, the place of infection, and yet a place of joy that I loved dearly. Again I had time on my hands while we waited to see what was going to happen to the worm farm in my brain, so I spent a lot of time over the following weeks reflecting on my experiences in Africa – the source of my current dance with death. I went there to serve selflessly, to make a difference if I could, and it seemed I was being punished for my sincere efforts.

What's up with that, God?

Chapter 4

Peace Corps Namibia

I remember leaving the United States totally unsure if I was doing the right thing. I was twenty-three and I knew I wanted to explore the world, help people and experience personal growth, and the U.S. Peace Corps seemed to promise all of that in a neat little package. All the other volunteers that I met seemed so excited, so sure. Some had been dreaming of doing this since they were eleven years old – Peace Corps Volunteer poster children. Me, I had gone into the Peace Corps office one afternoon on a whim to just get some information – and that led me all the way to Africa.

I had only heard of Namibia before by chance, or crazy synchronicity rather. In 1990 during my senior year in high school, I participated in a model United Nations in our world history class. I was assigned to act as the delegate for Namibia. I had to research the country, which had just gained its independence from apartheid South African rule earlier that year, and represent it in a mock UN conference which included high schools from all over the county. I never would have guessed that one day I might actually live in Namibia with the Oshikwanyama tribe, sleep in a hut, and eat goat and mohongu right out of a basket with the best of them. Although my friends never quite pronounced it right, forever calling it Nambia or Nabibia, I packed my backpack not knowing what in the world to expect and got on a plane.

It was a long flight to Namibia via England and South Africa. We were exhausted but excited, glued to the windows as the plane landed in the desert landscape. We all gasped as the plane went down the runway because for some reason it was flanked with wrecked planes along both sides. If someone had a fear of flying this was not the sight to see: wings over here, over there, passenger seats falling out of the belly of planes torn in two. It seemed like they had crashed right there on the runway and then were moved over to clear the way for the next plane to land. It was unsettling to behold. But alas, here we were.

I arrived in the capital, Windhoek, with seventy-two new volunteers who would be sent all over the country to serve in different capacities. The new government in Namibia asked for help with basic infrastructure, especially in the education system. And here we were, in our Teva sandals with overstuffed backpacks full of bug spray, Nalgene bottles, extra tampons and head lamps – ready to change the world.

They opened the door and we were all itching to get off the plane. But before we could even see the outside the heat entered the plane like a shock wave. It was November, summer in Namibia and the Namib Desert reaches unbearably hot temperatures, we quickly learned.

We exited the plane onto the runway itself. There was no floating hallway leading you into the airport. No people movers or escalators. We stepped right onto the tarmac and took in the arid, crimson, craggy landscape around us. Our group converged to sing the Namibian national anthem, something we had learned on the way, and we sang it with timid off-key voices. I would find out later that the Namibian people had clear melodious voices harmonizing effortlessly and always.

Namibia, land of the brave
Freedom fight we have won
Glory to their bravery
Whose blood waters our freedom
We give our love and loyalty
Together in unity

Contrasting beautiful Namibia
Namibia our country
Beloved land of savannas
Hold high the banner of liberty
Namibia our country
Namibia motherland
We love thee.

Powerful words, I thought, for a new country that had barely survived a difficult path to freedom.

The Namibians sent to greet and take us to our training site politely tried to hide their cringing faces and laughter at how poorly our group sang. Nonetheless they were impressed that we had learned their anthem and so they showed us their gratitude for honoring their country and culture in that way, and for coming to help them.

We went by bus to a small town an hour from the capital and spent the next two months taking classes in local language, Namibian culture, and technical training, such as how to work in Namibian secondary schools, complete with a model school set up with volunteer students on their summer break. We also had health classes, where we received innumerable immunization shots in our bums or listened to nurses and videos teach us how to take care of ourselves. The videos showed all the terrible things that could go wrong with our health, and what preventive measures to take to avoid getting all those rashes and scary diseases, including how to filter our water with Peace Corps–issued water filters. Even though the classes were taught by the most jovial nurses, this was not our favorite time of the week. We watched programs about worms that would grow in your blood vessels and crawl out of your calf slowly over days or weeks, and how to wrap the long worm around a pencil until it was finally out. If you pulled too hard it would rip and die with most of its body inside your leg and start to rot. Yummy. Or there were the worms that would crawl up a stream of urine and dive straight into the head of a man's penis. So never pee in a pool of water! Or how about those critters in the "drinking water" that would give you bouts of diarrhea so bad it could kill, or malaria – ugh. It was somewhat scary but we were still so excited to be there.

Two months after living like kids at summer camp, sleeping in small bunk beds and eating cafeteria food, we were shipped off to our assigned villages. Just like that. Sent to villages where no one really spoke English. Sent to villages where there were no roads, only bushes and stones used for navigation. Sent to villages where the food was unrecognizable by sight or smell. Villages that were far away from anyone and anything we knew.

We were divided by region and bussed to little motels in key towns around the country. The next morning our school superintendents were supposed to come pick us up individually and take us to our new homes. We had all grown quite close over those two months: seventy-two adventurous, service-oriented kindred spirits. The bus ride to the motel was full of laughter, tears, fears, anticipation – and car crashes. We passed so many car crashes on that eight-hour bus ride to northern Namibia. Once, a hearse passed us on the two-lane highway at an alarming speed. About an hour later we came upon an accident in which the same hearse had hit another car head on and the coffin came right through the front windshield on impact, decapitating the driver and passenger. We arrived at the motel shortly after seeing that, feeling very unsettled and nervous. I am not sure if any of us got much sleep.

The next morning my new superintendent came to pick up another volunteer and me. We greeted him in our carefully practiced Oshikwanyama, the language of the tribe I was going to live with, and he smiled at our efforts, delighted we were there. We rode in the back of his battered baby-blue pick-up truck enjoying the wind on our skin and in our hair, taking in the landscape, excited to start this new chapter of our lives.

Then we came upon another terrible car accident just moments after it happened. A station wagon packed with a family of five had flipped. The superintendent pulled over to the side of the road and told us to get out and help the people – he was going to get some assistance. The other volunteer and I got out and ran to the family, most of whom had been able to get out of the car and were wandering around in different directions stunned and injured. The father had been pulled out of the car by one of the family members and was lying on the ground next to the wrecked station wagon. He was dead already. The mother was barely hanging on, unconscious and hardly breathing. The older brother had his teeth broken in and his face was cut and bleeding badly. The sister was totally dazed, cut in various places with her dress torn and hanging off of her. She was wandering around bawling and yelling loudly about her dress. She seemed completely fixed on the fact that her skirt was ripped and that her slip was showing. I managed to help her get her dress back on, which quieted her down, and then approached the ten-year-old younger brother. He seemed to be unscathed but I could tell his heart was breaking as he watched his parents die right in front of him. I picked him up and just held him in my arms trying to comfort him, and tried to give him some sense of safety and love.

There were no ambulance services in these parts. No 9-1-1 to call. All of the vehicles that the superintendent tried to stop for help sped away, screaming something about the hospital holding them responsible for the family's wounds if they were to drive them there. They wanted no part of it. I was amazed as car after car drove by without lending a hand. I still to this day don't know why the superintendent didn't try to drive them to the hospital himself. Probably for the same reason everyone else refused. Finally a truck stopped and loaded the wounded and dead into the back of their vehicle and drove away towards the nearest hospital.

And all of a sudden, just like that, the family was gone, leaving their flipped station wagon, caused by a burst tire, lying in a field where it would probably stay for years to come, to rust, decay and crumble. We climbed back into the back of the truck and continued on our journey. Quiet. Not really noticing the fresh air any more.

It was the end of January when I arrived in Oshikango, my new home, and the middle of a very hot dry summer. I was driven through the bush to a fenced-in group of huts called a "homestead" a few minutes shy of the Angolan border. The huts were all made of stalk with thatched grass roofs and doors only as high as my chest, forcing me to duck quite low just to enter.

I was introduced to my new family. I was first introduced to Meme Kulu, which translates into "elderly, respected mother figure." She was 70 years old. Her feet were spread wide from walking barefoot in the sand all her life and the skin on the bottom was as thick as any shoe sole I have ever seen. She was stout and looked withered from the sun and a hard life, but her face was full of strength and fortitude. Her smile was wide, bearing a few white, crooked teeth and she seemed delighted that I was there. There were five children. Annika, a six-year-old girl; two boys, Dumeni and Silas, ages seven and eight, respectively; Ndeshi was nine and Letitia was ten. All of these children were related to Meme Kulu in some way or another and had lived on this farm since they were able to walk.

My homestead, owned by my host family, was a group of thirty-two huts surrounded by a fence and then surrounded by the fields they toiled over day in and day out. I originally thought that having thirty-two huts was quite extravagant but it turned out that it was pretty normal. The huts were small. You had to duck into each of them because the doors were only a few feet high yet you could stand up in the center. They were no more than six to ten feet in diameter with either a sand floor, which remained cool thanks to the roof and always felt good on bare feet, or a caked mud/cement floor. Some huts were for sleeping, some for food storage; two were kitchen huts used for cooking indoors and preparing food. One was strictly for drinking home-brew with guests. And some were decrepit and not used for anything.

Two of those huts belonged to me. I had a "summer hut" and a "winter hut." Sounds luxurious, doesn't it? The summer hut was a small round structure with walls made from the stalks of the grain that grew in the fields and a metal door that hung to the walls by string – there was no window. The roof was thatched grass and the floor was sand. The winter hut was made out of a mixture of packed clay and cement and had a roof of corrugated tin with a million nail holes in it that leaked like a sieve in the rainy season. The winter hut was more spacious and clean with walls that looked like normal walls to me, and a door that you could actually walk through instead of crouching low to enter. I chose to live in that one most of the time. But my God, it was as hot as an oven (it literally was a clay oven of sorts). The Peace Corps had supplied me with a gas fridge and stove with a rickety old table and two chairs in that winter hut. I graded most of my student's homework at this table by candlelight. I also had a bedroom with a cot covered by mosquito netting and a tall wardrobe. I decorated my two rooms with artwork that I made and flowers when they were in bloom, and came to love them dearly.

The shower that I used was no more than a three-by-three square of cement on the ground with shoulder-high homemade brick walls. I was naked inside this enclosure while I bathed, using a bucket or the solar shower I brought from the States, but could easily see into the fields around me. I saw my students from school or other villagers walk by and they would greet me. I knew they could not see me below the shoulders but my naked body was exposed to the fresh air and I felt as if they could see everything. It took some getting used to.

I had no running water in either of my huts. Nobody had running water in these parts. There were only two taps that I knew of that served this village of thousands of people. They used to only have well water, but when the South African troops occupied the country they set up pipes that brought water up from a town about an hour's drive away. When the troops left, the villagers began to use the spigots and the wells were abandoned and eventually not used anymore. Kids and women lined up at the two taps all day, every day, filling large buckets, putting them on their heads and skillfully walking back home – not spilling a drop. I, too, filled my buckets but carried them clumsily back to my hut by the handles, spilling water everywhere. I eventually developed the courage to carry groceries and books on my head but never these crazy big buckets of water. Once I saw an elderly woman in her seventies or eighties carry a kitchen table on her head, upside down so the legs pointed up in the air, with four wooden chairs balanced on top of the table – along with two large buckets of water. She walked effortlessly in the soft sand with this heavy load on her head, turning left and right to greet her friends, her spine straight and strong.

At home I used a regular toilet that the family had placed over a latrine hole they had dug into the sand. I brought water with me in a bucket and after using the pot I poured the water from the bucket into the toilet to flush it all down. It literally went from the toilet bowl straight into the huge dirt hole below, slowly filling the space as large as my bedroom, dug just for me. From time to time the family that I lived with used this toilet too, although not much. They used old magazines and paper to wipe with. I once looked down next to the toilet to see a full head shot of JFK from a magazine. He wore a nice suit and a bright handsome smile. I apologized to him. I knew where he was headed.

I perspired so much in the relentless heat that my clothes were continually stinky and soaked with sweat. When I washed clothes I often used too much soap to hide the stink and too little water to rinse since it was only available by bucket-fetching. This, I learned, was not a good combination.

I often went jogging for exercise and the Namibian people would yell out at me, "What is wrong, miss? What are you running from? Who is chasing you?" Their life was so physically demanding and draining just to survive that the thought of expending energy unnecessarily was complete-ly foreign to them. The adults would shake their head in both amusement and bewilderment, and I always had a gaggle of little children running behind me giggling endlessly at this crazy white woman running through the sand for no apparent reason. "Oshilumbu! Oshilumbu!" they would yell with laughter meaning: "White person, white person!"

One particular day during the start of the rainy season, I started jog-ging. The falling rain began to relieve the heat that traveled in waves up from the sand in every direction. It felt so cooling to my skin, so refresh-ing. So I just kept on running. I looked over and saw an old man sitting in the shelter of his hut. He was looking at me and was laughing hysterically. Since it was a common occurrence to have people laugh at me when I ran, I just greeted him and jogged on in the rain but he seemed to be laughing a little more than usual.

After a couple of minutes I happened to glance down, and as a result of too much soap and too little rinsing, plus the rain and friction from run-ning, my shorts were foaming like crazy in my crotch. I had huge sudsy white foaming bubbles gushing from between my legs front and back. I immediately wiped it away but it just kept coming. If I slowed to a walk the foam production slowed a little but there was no way to stop it completely unless I stood absolutely still in the pouring rain in the middle of the des-ert – with a ninety-year-old man laughing his brains out at the oshilumbu.

So, I just kept on running. I ran and ran until I got home – foaming all the way. Luckily not many people were out in the rain. They used the rainy times to do indoor chores. But I was sure that the old man would tell many villagers about the funny oshilumbu with the foaming crotch, laughing all the while.

The village kids woke at 4 a.m. to pound the grain into flour to avoid the sun and the 125 degree-plus heat of midday. And they sang. They sang and pounded the grain with creative rhythms that made music of the work. Then they went to school all day, came home and worked until sundown and beyond if the moon was full. Yet they sang and laughed and danced all the time.

Everyone sang in this village. They could harmonize with each other as if they had practiced together for years. I remember a time at the model school during my training when the kids sang the Namibian national anthem every morning before school. They had perfect pitch and three-part harmonies blended together effortlessly and beautifully. When the American volunteers were prompted to sing our national anthem someone finally piped up to start it, but she began on a very high note that later sent the highest notes in the middle of the anthem way up into soprano land – and we were so off-key. It was embarrassing. The kids were looking at each other as if to say, "Are they doing that on purpose?," trying hard not to laugh.

Even their language is sung, not spoken. The Oshikwanyama language has a high ratio of vowels and although it is not a tonal language, such as Mandarin Chinese, they sing it like a fluid joyful song. Until someone is upset, then it is still a song but has a lot of added syllables of "tsss" and breathy "uhhh" sounds.

I spent my weekend days learning and speaking Oshikwanyama, especially with Annika, the precious little six-year-old that lived on my homestead. She was very small for her age and I could easily pick her up and put her on my shoulders or back. We walked around with me pointing to object after object asking, "How do you say this in Oshikwanyama?" Star. Tree. Flower. Bird. She spoke no English, none of the family members did, and when I got there I spoke very little of her language despite the twice-daily classes the Peace Corps had put me through. Although she was just a child she loved that she could be my teacher. I truly had the experience that language is not necessary to play or connect with a child. She giggled and dressed up in crazy outfits, something I had also loved to do as a child, and we ran and chased each other around. She was a source of sunshine every day.

Chapter 5

Teaching Life

The first day I went to school I wove my way past the bushes and rocks that I was supposed to use as landmarks, hoping to remember them for the long walk home. But I was distracted thinking about everything else I needed to remember for the day.

When I arrived at school the first thing to do is to say hello, an important cultural event that I didn't want to forget. I did my best to remember the greeting that took many minutes to say. But everyone seemed to have time for this and they were patient with me. I never saw anyone there in a hurry.

I greeted all the teachers in a row. It seemed to take forever but thankfully they seemed please by my efforts. I would begin:

"Walelepo, mey-mey." ("Good morning, Ma'am. You are good?")

She replied, "Eh," sung as three syllables. ("Yes, I am good.")

I would say, "Oshili nawa?" ("You are really good?")

"Eh," she replied again. ("Yes, I am really good.")

"Oshili shili nawa?" I asked. ("You are really, really good?")

"Eh. Walelepo. Mey-mey." ("Yes, I am really, really good. Good morning, miss. You are good?") And she then enquired if I was really good – really, really good.

I replied that I was.

Then finally we both said, "Ee-ah-lo, tangee uney-ney." ("Thank you. Thank you very much.")

I went through this dialogue with all twenty-two teachers every morning – one at a time! It took forever. But at least I knew that they were all good.

Really good.

Really, really good.

Every day.

That afternoon I tried my best to make it back home using those rocks and bushes as landmarks, but I quickly became lost. All the rocks and bushes looked alike! The twenty-minute walk became forty minutes – and then an hour. I started having fears that I would be roaming around in the African bush overnight and never find my homestead. I was imagining an article coming out in the newspaper: "Peace Corps volunteer dies of thirst in the village of Oshikango. Her body was found facedown in the sand with a million flies on her back. The poor girl didn't even last a day." But then, all of a sudden, I saw my homestead in the distance. I made it back to my hut just fine. It turned out I had been circling it for an hour. And being the only white person in the village everyone knew who I was and where I was staying. Anyone could have taken me right home.

When I walked into my hut I drank some water out of my official Peace Corps–issued water filter and glanced on the ground. I saw that my solid deodorant that had fallen on its side that morning had melted in the intense heat and was a huge white puddle on the floor. My cassette tapes had also melted and all the plastic baggies felt wet and sticky. I learned that I had to keep everything remotely melt-able in my Peace Corps–issued gas-run refrigerator. I sure did miss the deodorant.

School was really enjoyable. I taught ninth and tenth grades, with sixty kids in each class piled on top of one another in a small clay room (again, an oven which was so hot in the summer it was almost unbearable). My thermometer, which was kept inside in the school library in the shade, would top out at 125 degrees Fahrenheit every single day during those long summer months. I am not sure how hot it actually got since my thermometer didn't go any higher.

But my classrooms seemed roomy compared to the lower grades. They were pushing a hundred students per room. Children were everywhere in those elementary school grades: under desks, on top of them, with kids all over the floor, and much of the time they did not have any pens, pencils or books.

At school the toilets were a different story than the one at my home. There were no western toilets here. Knee-high circular walls were built up from the ground straight over the latrine pits. The roof of the three stalls that served 1,000 plus students and staff had blown off in a storm months before I arrived, and during my whole two years there the roof was never repaired. The sunlight was free to shine down those holes crawling with thousands of maggots and other things. The metal doors barely hung onto the cement walls by old rusted wire. I was so careful to never touch anything in there and tried to hover far away from the maggoty holes while I peed, hoping that my students and little children couldn't see through the gaping holes on either side of the doors. I think they did though. It was always an uncomfortable adventure to use the bathroom there, and despite careful use of my Peace Corps–issued water filter, I had to use the bathroom way more than normal. Yikes.

I was nervous in front of my classes as I tried to take the attendance while attempting somehow to remember the names that were a crazy string of unfamiliar syllables. They always laughed at my pronunciation. I spoke English with the kids very slowly like I had practiced but the kids that came to our model school near the capital city had much better English skills than the village kids did. I learned that quickly. There were a handful of boys who understood most of what I said. A handful of kids, mostly girls, who understood nothing I said. And the rest got about half of it, I guessed.

I was teaching math and science to grades nine and ten. Until 1990, the country had been under apartheid rule and the South African government decided what they were and were not allowed to learn in their schools. Math was a subject that they decided was not necessary. English was another. So in 1990 when Namibia's first independent government was formed, they decided to put math education back in the schools and chose English as their official language; a common language to unite the numerous and extremely different tribes whom each had their own language. They wanted a language that wasn't the official language of their oppressors, Afrikaans, although a lot of Namibians could speak it. And they wanted a language that would allow them to interact more internationally. English was the logical choice. However after that announcement in 1990, it was as if all of a sudden everyone was supposed to speak English – with no teachers or CDs to play, and no educational TV programs to watch in these little villages that had no electricity. So most of the old villagers resigned never to learn it while most of the kids in my village saw it as a key to their escape as they grew older. They learned it as best they could despite the fact that the Namibian-born English teacher could barely speak it and the principal of the school could not speak it at all.

Up until 1990 no one in northern Namibia had taken math above a second grade level. In 1991 they had math classes put in the schools from grades one to twelve. It was time to choose math teachers but no one had ever learned it. All of a sudden people were randomly chosen to teach math in every grade. As an example, the grade nine's math teacher at our school stepped into the class with a new government-issued math book trying to teach what he did not understand. The students had never taken math before so trying to jump into grade nine math topics without knowing how to subtract was a nightmare. From what I observed too, the teachers were so embarrassed and flustered about not understanding the material that they would not allow the students to ask questions because they could never answer them and they feared being made to look the fool. And respect from the students was very important to these people.

The intentions were grand and so textbooks were given out to all the schools, but the challenge was a huge one. Hence, when the Peace Corps asked the Namibian government what kind of help they wanted, they asked them to send math and English teachers. I arrived and quickly figured out that my tenth graders, some of whom were older than me, couldn't subtract if you needed to borrow, couldn't do long division or work with fractions. And I was supposed to be teaching geometry and algebra? Their English was so poor that word problems were next to impossible even if they could do the math. Where should I begin?

Well, I just started. I taught during their normally scheduled periods. I taught after school and those that could come would come. I figured out that often teachers would skip their own classes and drink home brew in the library or saunter off to the bank. Although this would never be condoned in America, this was common practice in this culture and was not looked down upon by our principal. This meant that when teachers didn't show up the kids just sat there talking, and if the kids left the room they got in trouble. So I took up those periods, too. Sometimes those kids would have hours on end of math lessons, and they worked quietly until their brains would start to melt in the heat and they couldn't concentrate anymore. Although they were living in a harsh environment with few resources to help them develop and feel empowered, they learned quickly and joyfully.

It was amazing to teach them things that I took for granted, like the fact that the sun was bigger than the earth. Oh, they fought me on that one. They took me outside, laughing at me and pointed to the sun and said, "Mey-mey, look at that circle. It is so small. How can it be bigger than this big earth we are standing on? How can the sun be bigger than the large moon that hangs in the same sky?" Then I took them into the classroom and gave one of the kids a quarter and a basketball. I told him to hold the quarter in front of his face while I walked the basketball across the room. I asked him which one looked bigger to his eye, the quarter an inch away or the basketball far away. It was in these moments, when they began to think more abstractly and expand their understanding of our universe, that I lit up. So did they.

Later that week I taught them about eclipses and how they worked. I believe I used the same basketball (Donated by Nike because of some letters I sent off asking for donations. The boys loved those basketballs more than anything.) and other smaller balls to show the mechanics of an eclipse. I had no idea we were due for one but that same week we had an almost full eclipse of the sun. Everyone in the village was surprised and thought dark spirits were there but all my students jumped up and explained to their families what was happening. The next day at school they could not stop talking about it, telling me how many people they taught what was happening with the earth and sun. My degree in astrophysics was good for something after all. But within limits.

Another thing that blew me away was that nobody there knew that man had walked on the moon. When I told them that small scientific fact they all started laughing hysterically, elbowing each other with smiles on their faces like I was being totally ridiculous. No way were they going to swallow that one.

I began to grow attached to my students. Their country had gone through a long war and there were students with limbs blown off from land mines and boys who had seen more death than I could even imagine. Many of them were older than the normal age for ninth and tenth grade. I was just out of college, so although our education levels were incredibly different, some of them were about my age or even a few years older than me. They seemed younger though, by far. They wore student uniforms which made them all look like school kids and most of them had not been out of the village. They had never seen a set of stairs, an airplane, a shopping mall; some of them had never even talked on the phone. They seemed so young when it came to life experience in some ways but surviving war and hard physical labor had toughened them up, too. I came to love them all. They were my students, but they were also my friends and I wanted so badly for them to succeed.

The hunger these kids felt for education was there because they wanted out. Out of their simple village life. I spoke with them at great length about how precious their own cultural ways were and how amazing it was to have a tribe, a sense of real belonging to a people with ancient practices. But they wanted none of it. They wanted "things": tennis shoes and watches and cars and money. And they wanted the freedom to move away, which education would provide.

Apparently that's just how the Namibian culture works in small villages. When you get old enough to move away, around age eighteen, they jump at the chance to escape the harsh subsistence farm life to go get a job in a larger town nearby. Sex is rampant and birth control is not usually used, despite all the sex education and propaganda showered onto the villagers by non-profit groups, though mostly for HIV prevention. But rumor has it that in those small villages, if you get HIV all you have to do is sleep with a virgin and it will go away. As a result, young girls often get pregnant quickly and don't have the finances or the maturity to take care of the child, so the child is then sent back to the homestead. The grandparents usually love this because although it is another mouth to feed, the work that the child can contribute to cultivating the fields usually outweighs what they can eat. So many of the homesteads are inhabited by grandparents, lots of kids, nursing mothers, and teenagers that are not yet finished with secondary school.

Some of the older kids are told to stay home from school to help in the fields or tend the goats. This turned out to be a great thing for me as a teacher. The kids in school had to fight to be there so they were good students. Couple that with the fact that with an education they could escape the village life, get a job somewhere and start buying fancy jeans and hair spray. They all dreamt of this. And for these reasons, although it hurt my heart as it became clear to me, it also meant that I had virtually no discipline problems in the classroom, which was an amazing blessing.

When I first arrived in Namibia I often found myself in conversation with other new volunteers about what we were even doing there to begin with. Most of us were young, idealistic and were there to teach. We knew we wanted to help in some way and that Namibia had asked for teachers. But it weighed on us whether we were actually needed there after all. At that stage, school was not enforced. And for many years previously, the South African government kept them from being educated at all, even if they wanted to be. So these kids had freedom that they had fought for, lost friends and family members for, and they were now given the choice if they wanted an education. That was why I was there. I was there to grant them that freedom, to give them the basic right of learning things about the world, to do with it what they would, even if it broke my heart to see them use it to leave the ways of the village.

Eventually I found peace about being a teacher there. On one hand I was watching their culture disappear in a sad way right in front of my eyes. Plastic bags were introduced to the village and they became a status symbol of sorts. People felt important if they had things inside a plastic bag because it meant that they had the money to buy something. And as the village people were used to everything being biodegradable, they just threw the bags on the ground when they were through with them. In the heart of the village market plastic bags littered the landscape everywhere. They hung on trees and were all over the ground. It was terrible. There was a slow but steady infiltration of materialism and all that sadly went with it.

So I resolved to dedicate two years of my life in service to help them get the education that they were striving for, as I practiced non-attachment to what they did with it.

I worked hard at the school but I also had quite a bit of time for myself too. School was over by two in the afternoon and life was quiet and spacious there. I was deep into my path of seeking meaning for my life. I wrote in my journal and spent long hours in quiet meditation and thought. I began writing a self-portrait of sorts, each syllable a brush stroke painting the Me that I could see at the moment: who I was, who I wanted to be, what I believed and why. I had no distractions: no electricity; no phone; no email; no television or radio and no bills to pay; just endless days of sunshine, moonlight, and candles to light my way during the nights of the new moon. It was a time of hard work with my students but much rest for my soul. I cherished the time spent in nature with no traffic, stress or pressure to keep up with anyone or anything.

During my contemplations I put quite a bit of focus on what I wanted to be "when I grew up." I absolutely loved being a schoolteacher in Namibia but a great deal of that had to do with the freedom I had in the classrooms and the lack of politics. I did not have to turn in my lesson plans or go to staff meetings or do paperwork of any kind, and my students were unique and wonderful with virtually no discipline issues. I knew I would not have a similar experience in the States. In fact, I was quite sure it would be just the opposite.

My other big interest in life was medicine, and in those early months in my village I began to volunteer in a couple of nearby hospitals in the afternoons. I began to visit all sorts of patients in the wards just to keep them company. Once, when I first started at the hospital I came across a young girl I guessed was about six years old. She was tiny, bald and in bad shape. I was told that she had tuberculosis of the spine. Her mother had taken her to the local witch doctor for healing when the first symptoms showed up. The witch doctor worked with her for a long time expelling spirits and doing whatever it is that they do but it didn't work, and as a last resort she had landed in the hospital. It turned out that she was twelve years old, not six, her growth stunted by her illness. She was completely paralyzed from the waist down at this point. The doctor said that if the mother had brought her to the hospital when the symptoms first started she probably would have been fine. I was still new to the village and my language skills were very rough around the edges but we were able to communicate about simple things. I brought her crayons and books and tried not to make faces when I saw her infected bedsores. One day she disappeared. I was never able to find out for sure what had happened to her.

I also fell in love with physical medicine. I was lucky. I came across physiotherapists from all over the world who had come to work in the hospitals in different capacities and they were all happy to have my help. The hospitals were always incredibly overcrowded and understaffed. One woman I found near the end of my stay was from the Netherlands. She had been there for a few years and was totally fluent in Oshidonga, the tribal language of the people where she lived, a little over a hundred kilometers from my village. I liked working with her. She described to me what was going on with the patients and gave me instructions on how to help. And she made such a difference in their lives.

One of the daughters of the elderly woman I lived with was married to a Nigerian healer. I am not sure how they met, but he moved to Namibia to be with her and they lived in a town not far away. He was on a mission to collect the wisdom of the traditional healers in the surrounding villages, to begin a school for the youth to learn the ancient healing ways. He was gathering information on herbal medicine, rituals, ceremonies and any other kind of medicine the witch doctors (their word for healer) used. I would go visit him often and ask him about how the

Nigerian healers worked with people. I would tour through the school that he started and see the strange plants and concoctions of all different colors brewing in jars. The people there were not very open to an oshilumbu learning from a witch doctor, but I did learn quite a bit from this man and was fascinated by the practices and ideas of traditional healing.

When the end of my stay was approaching, I knew I needed to figure out what to do next, where in the world to move to and what to do for work or school. I searched with an earnest heart for clarity about my role in this world. I prayed for a clear calling. And over time an answer became crystal clear to me. By the time I left my homestead, I knew to the core of my being that my role in this world was to be a healer.

I had no idea at the time how encompassing this path would be for me. I thought it meant that I would go to medical school and work with Doctors Without Borders. But I learned over the years that being a "doctor" and being a "healer" are not necessarily the same thing. And that being a healer is a very hard road. The universe had more in store for me than just learning the science of medicine from a textbook.

As the weeks in my village came to a close, I was given a gift as a token of appreciation. His name was George, I decided. He was a goat as high as my waist and very fat. I was meant to kill him and eat him. This was a huge gift both in symbolism and in physical size. Goats were a staple in the diet and one could feed many people. They were not cheap, especially one this big. I was honored but a little disturbed knowing what was to become of him. I was having a going-away gathering the following week and decided to save him for that. I had him on a leash of sorts made of rope and I kept him outside my hut tied to a post. I hung out with him daily, fed him and gave him water. I actually became a little attached to George, I have to say.

Let me note here that the Oshikwanyama people did not have a word for "pet" in their language. The idea of keeping an animal purely for companionship was not an idea they had ever considered. We had a dog on our homestead, a dog that I would pet and feed sometimes and that dog followed me everywhere, running so close to my heels when I went jogging that I tripped over him constantly. Apparently no one ever pet the dogs – they were used for security purposes only and barked when someone, especially a stranger, approached the homestead. That was their purpose. And every animal had a purpose. One day after coming back from being away for a long weekend I noticed that the dog wasn't around. I asked the kids in Oshikwanyama, "Where's the dog?" They shrugged and said, "Oh, we ate him," as if it was nothing at all. "The dog was getting too old to bark much. He got too quiet." And that was that.

In the middle of my service, one of my fellow Peace Corps Volunteers was leaving Namibia. She worked with primary school teachers and her contract was nearing an end. She asked me if I would like her collection of school/art supplies she had been collecting: egg cartons, paper, random trash that could be transformed creatively into art. I enthusiastically accepted her gift. The students at my school had precious little school supplies in general and it was going to be fun providing this for them to work with. She had a truck and came by my school one day to say that she had dropped the supplies off by my door at the homestead.

When I got there, there was a heap – no, a mountain of white plastic bags full of strange art supplies. I opened the door to my winter hut and threw bag after bag inside into a huge pile. The next day a relative of the family came by and asked me if I liked the kitten he had left for me. I had been asking my memekulu if it was all right if I got a kitten (as a pet) and she said it was fine. Her son, trying to be thoughtful, wanted to get a kitten for me as a surprise. "What kitten?" I asked. He said, "I left it in front of your door in a white bag yesterday!" I felt a rock inside my belly when I realized what had happened. I rushed into the room with the mountain of white bags and found a large potato sack amongst the other white plastic bags. Sure enough there was a wiggling creature inside. I carefully opened the long white bag, stuck my arm all the way inside to find a tiny fuzzy warm body at the bottom. I put my fingers around its belly and started to pull it out. When it reached broad daylight the kitten made a horrific screech and dug its claws deeply into my chest and used that as leverage to leap across the room to the window and ran away. I never saw it again! I was only left with bloody claw marks on my chest as a souvenir. Of all the days to leave a white bag at my door! I never got another pet after that. Until George.

But George's days were numbered. I knew that. So I tried to give him a comfortable home until 'the day' came. And eventually that day did come. According to their customs if you receive an animal like that to slaughter and eat you had to be the one to "do the honors." So on the morning of my going-away feast, Annika, who was then eight years old, came into my hut and told me it was time to start preparing the goat. They led me to a shelter behind our homestead specifically built to slaughter animals in and gave me a knife.

I looked at the knife with a conflicting feeling in my belly, and a little concern. The knife was a small and very dull steak knife. It turned out it was the best one they had but it didn't seem like it was sharp enough to do the job well. It was literally the size of a butter knife but a little pointy on the top. I expressed my concern and they tried to sharpen it with a rock, which did nothing. They gave it back to me and I looked at it, looked at George, and bowed my head. The four children held George down on his side, securing his feet together on the ground as another child held his head back. They motioned down to his throat.

It was time for me to begin cutting.

I had a silent conversation with George at that moment – my spirit with his. I thanked him for his life, thanked him for feeding so many people and thanked Spirit for giving him to nourish us.

Then I took a deep breath and went to his throat with this crappy knife and just cut and cut and cut.

It took a long time. It felt like it was hours. But I also know that the long seconds and minutes I experienced weren't in real time.

He struggled against me but the kids knew what they were doing and were able to hold him down well. I finally cut through his tough skin into the cords that carried his breath to his lungs. When those went and the blood flowed long enough he became still. I felt his life leave him right under my hands and I thanked him. It was a very sacred experience for me to take the life of an animal with my own hand while honoring his being. I felt connected to him in a way that I had never experienced with an animal before.

I was then told to cut a long line down the skin covering his belly, then two lines from leg to leg and then to fold his skin back to reveal his inner organs. The kids dug in to deal with the innards and cut the muscle tissue up for meat. We cooked him over a fire, the only means of cooking we had, and used every single bit of him. Even his intestines were cleaned out and draped from the fence to drain and dry. They even kept his skin and used the hide later. He fed about eighty-five people that day. He was a big guy.

I allowed my female students to take home most of my clothes that I had worn the past couple of years. They lit up as if it was Christmas. There was a feast, a lot of smiles and a spontaneous speech from me that was translated by one of the teachers at my school. This translation option allowed me to speak freely and more quickly, expressing ideas I wouldn't know how to say in Oshikwanyama.

I was totally surprised to hear what came out of my mouth that day. It was a message straight from my heart. I spoke of equality and personal empowerment and how grateful I was to have had that experience with them. I wanted to share how much I loved them all and how much I learned from them; how my world had shifted and how thankful I was to each of them for accepting me into their village. I spoke at great lengths about equality and felt that having that message come from a white person's mouth was very powerful for them given what they had endured under South African oppression. I had been a living example for them that not all white people were prejudiced or cruel.

It was an epic day.

After hugs were given and good-byes were said people started drifting home, walking through the sand, using the bushes, trees and the setting sun as navigational guides just as they always did and would continue to do – I hoped with all my heart.

Chapter 6

Out of Africa

It is strange for a human being to be given a possible time limit on one's life. What does one think about? What does one do? As I was taking the experimental drug cocktail and waiting to see if I was going to live or die, I spent those three weeks thinking about some of my favorite memories, especially the two years I served in the Peace Corps and the travels that followed. When I left Africa, I had many adventures that gave me such joy. There were so many magical experiences that I had when I surrendered to spontaneous travel. However, while thinking about those times, a heaviness came over me too. Was I ever going to experience adventures like that again?

When you leave your host country after serving in the Peace Corps they will give you either a one-way ticket home or you can get the cash value of the ticket and independently get yourself home. I opted for the latter option. It was peak season approaching Christmas time so the cost of a one-way ticket from Namibia to Denver, Colorado was enough to get me a big fat round-the-world ticket instead, with some money back to boot.

For the next several months I traveled extensively through Ethiopia, Italy, Nepal, Thailand and Bali – a welcome contrast to being rooted in southern Africa for over two years. I was able to travel through many of the surrounding countries during the school breaks while in Namibia, but it was completely new for me to have the freedom to look at the entire globe and go where I wanted. It had been a long standing dream of mine that I wasn't sure would ever come true. I lived in constant gratitude and wide-eyed wonder, no matter how tired I was or cramped it was on a crazy bus. I thought it was all absolutely wonderful.

In Ethiopia I stayed with a family of three sisters in Addis Ababa. One of my Peace Corps Volunteer friends knew the sisters well and had arranged for me and another PCV to stay with them. Upon our arrival they made us a huge feast and proceeded to talk me into getting extensions braided into my short hair. One of the sisters went that afternoon to get the fake dark brown hair that matched my own and that evening the three of them sat around me and taught me Amharic, answered my questions about their life and culture, and proceeded to braid my hair with long extensions so tightly that a clear liquid oozed through my hair follicles. It hurt so much I could hardly talk while they were doing it. Luckily, they were excited to have us there so they did most of the talking. I sat with a grimace on my face that I passed off for a smile of sorts.

Every mealtime they fed us the most amazing Ethiopian fare. Each meal was accompanied by injera, the staple flat pancake that they use to mop up all the magical tasty side dishes they would prepare. In the morning it was injera with eggs. In the afternoon it was injera with vegetables and sometimes meat. The same went for dinner. It was much like the Namibian people with their mohongu, except the dishes served with it were more flavorful and diverse in Ethiopia.

One afternoon they tried to teach me how to make the injera. It looked simple enough, pouring frothy fermented bean batter onto the large round burner that was designed specifically for making injera. I watched the sisters make pancake after pancake and it seemed like they just poured the batter in a spiral fashion onto the burner. The burner was huge, around two and a half feet in diameter. So in order to pour an even amount of batter over it they started on the outside and poured the batter around and around until they hit the center. It looked so easy!

However it took a more steady and practiced hand than mine. I managed to make a terrible mess of it, causing me to laugh so hard that the rest of my batter pouring was even more ungraceful, producing a pancake that looked more like a strange piece of modern art. The sisters laughed uncontrollably, but it was a fantastic bonding experience – even if we didn't speak each other's language.

My traveling companion was a very tall and beautiful man. He had long wavy brown hair that he usually wore in a ponytail at the back of his head, sported a beard and mustache and was clearing six foot seven easily. He stood out so much on the streets of Ethiopia that we always had a multitude of children following us shouting, "Jesus! Jesus!" I hadn't noticed prior to that day, but he did look like Jesus – and his towering height added a magical quality to his presence in that environment. We had learned a little of their language and he would constantly raise his hand up to the kids and say, "Hello, hello!," wearing big smiles. After a few days we realized that we had both gotten the words for "hello" and "thank you" mixed up so the whole time the kids were following him and yelling praises he was raising one hand to the air saying, "Thank you, thank you!," thus encouraging even more praise.

We both wanted to travel to northern Ethiopia near the Eritrean border, but war had broken out between the two countries right when we got there. So we decided to travel south instead and showed up unannounced at a Peace Corps Volunteer's house. We were welcomed in, holding steadfast to the PCV open-door policy, as it is customary for a Peace Corps Volunteer to welcome another Peace Corps Volunteer into their home no matter where they are from. It is not required by the Peace Corps, it is just a kindred spirit kind of agreement that the volunteers themselves had developed. I never had a volunteer come to Oshikango – it was not a common travel destination — but I loved this freedom and opportunity to go to small villages and already have an in. We were introduced to her Ethiopian boyfriend and shown around their village. We learned that roadside ping-pong is a huge phenomenon all over Ethiopia, something that continued to fascinate me even after seeing the millionth ping-pong table in the middle of nowhere surrounded by people of all ages.

We then visited the Rastafarian complex in the southern part of the country. As we entered the complex, a man invited us into his home. We were offered a huge joint, which we both declined, and just sat and chatted with these folks about Rastafarianism. They had little framed signs every-where that said: "Read a chapter of the Bible every day." Ethiopia's king Tafari (king translates to "Ras" in Amharic) was regarded as the second coming of Christ. This king promised to bring the people of Jamaica back to Africa, and had set aside a huge portion of land in southern Ethiopia so they could come back to their "motherland." One day, I was told, there had been a long drought in Jamaica. Ras Tafari stepped off a plane and the minute his foot touched the ground it began to rain. This convinced many that he was a miracle worker and a living miracle himself.

Many Jamaicans were given passage on ships to return to Africa. This land, enveloped by Ethiopia, had a similar climate as Jamaica and still be-longed to the Rastafarians. It was like a country within a country, exempt from Ethiopian law, especially those regarding marijuana. Everyone I met there was extremely friendly, ready to share their beliefs and lifestyle but never trying to push it on anyone. I felt welcome and amazed.

I then flew directly from Ethiopia to Italy to meet my father and his wife. They often traveled there for vacation and it was now the time of the Carnival festival. It was February, and although it was incredibly hot in Ethiopia it was freezing in Italy with white snow covering the ground like a soft blanket. I went through a bit of culture shock going from one of the hottest, poorest countries, with some of the thinnest and blackest-skinned people, straight into a place full of overweight, rich and indulgent white people with extravagance dripping off the fingers of seemingly everyone, at least by comparison. People flaunted masks costing more than what some Ethiopians made in their entire lives – many times over. It was very difficult to adjust to. A mind trip. But it was fun to see my father and experience life with him in a different culture. I ate lots of amazing rich food. Oh, so much pasta, butter and delicious sauces! And yet I felt a distance between everyone there and myself, including my family. How could anyone possibly understand my experience in Africa over the past two and a half years? It was more than I could explain and too difficult to talk about so I just let it be – inside me.

I left my father and flew to Nepal and spent quite a bit of time there, first traveling into the middle of the mountains to live at a yoga ashram. I had never done yoga in my life and was always curious about it. This place was full on. We woke at four or five in the morning, spent hours doing cleansing yoga as we poured warm water up our noses and flushed our sinuses out onto the grass. We meditated several times a day, sometimes for hours at a time, and chanted and practiced asana (the poses) in the afternoon. We spent part of each day in silence and ate very interesting food meant to cleanse our bodies. After finishing the immersion I had signed up for, I was thankful for the crazy and intense experience, but I decided that yoga was a little much for me and so I left.

I decided to hike the beautiful Annapurna circuit. I was traveling alone and I thought that hiking in the Himalayan mountains would be a daunting affair. I imagined being in the wilderness with no map, no compass, only scraggly rocks with no knowledge of how to get to my destination. I was scared of getting lost and starving to death at high altitudes. So I hired a guide while I was in the capital city, which wasn't hard to arrange since they were advertised at every street corner. I met my guide the next day, and this little magical man named Balaji and I traveled to the base of the Annapurna circuit the next day. When we arrived at the base of the trail and took a look, I hung my head and laughed. The circuit

I was meant to follow wasn't a hidden trail going through the wilderness and rocks but a wide cobblestone path with donkeys being led up and down pulling impossible weights, with loads of tourists and many Nepali people walking as well. It was as wide as a road and I realized I had been duped into thinking I needed a guide, a common tourist trap that I had ignorantly fallen for. But I had already paid for his services for ten days – it was a done deal.

Balaji was a few years older than I was and at least a foot shorter. We sat over dinner the night before we were meant to start the trail and I asked him, over my dal and rice, what weddings were like in Nepal. The Ethiopian sisters had taken me to their cousin's wedding and I absolutely loved the pomp and circumstance that weddings can be in different cultures. Balaji sighed and said, "Oh, my sister is getting married in about a week, but I can't go. I got this job to take you trekking and I really needed the money so I will miss it." I couldn't believe my ears, and leaned over and said, "Balaji, this trail is so easy to follow I can easily do this by myself. If you think it would be OK for me to come, I would much rather go with you to your sister's wedding and you can keep the money for being my guide!" He smiled from ear to ear, and just like that, we decided to ditch the Annapurnas and head to his tiny mountaintop village.

We took bus after bus, sometimes riding in the back next to goats and chickens, sometimes on the very roof when the inside was full; buses that rocked back and forth as they zoomed down dirt roads full of potholes. It felt like they tipped onto two wheels while zooming around the tight corners. Perhaps it was just because I was on top holding on for dear life and my mind exaggerated the details. For the Nepali people this kind of travel was normal – except for having a white woman riding on the top of the bus with them.

After we got off the last bus in the middle of nowhere, we hiked through the fields then put our backpacks onto the tops of our heads while we waded through a waist-deep river. We climbed up the other side through more fields before we began the ascent up a steep but small mountain that was terraced with rice paddies. There was a tiny ancient-looking man stooped over a tool used to create the rice paddies, and upon meeting him I asked Balaji if I could try. They both laughed and gave me the tool. I felt what it was like to hold this sickle-like implement and till the ground. As the man showed me the motions, I could tell that he had done this for his entire life and I wondered what that life must have been like, so different from my own.

We continued up the mountain until we reached a group of houses and met Balaji's family. Everyone was quiet and a little sullen. Balaji explained that this was because they were going to lose the daughter that was getting married the next day. According to tradition the man and his wedding party comes to the bride's family home for the wedding and then carry her back to his village, which in this case was a full eight hours walk away. I was told that the bride hardly ever sees her family after her wedding day.

It was past dark and I was shown a ladder that led to an attic of sorts where I was to sleep. I climbed up and put my sleeping bag and mat on the wooden floor and fell into an easy deep sleep. What seemed like a short time later I was awakened by the sound of drums, singing, flutes and merriment. I strained to see where it was coming from. It didn't sound like it was from the homestead where I was staying, but I was afraid of missing out on what seemed to be a great celebration and I couldn't figure out the real source of all the noise. So I ended up falling back asleep after a while, but then woke up to someone licking my cheek and breathing into my ear.

At first when I was still in a dream-state, I went back in time in my mind and thought that it was my boyfriend from college loving on me in bed and kissing my ear. But as the loud breathing and sticky tongue kept going, I jerked out of my slumber only to find two huge eyes looking at me curiously, with a huge tongue reaching down periodically to see how I tasted. It took me a second to realize I was looking into the eyes of a large cow standing over me checking me out very intimately. I found out later that the families in Nepal take small calves up ladders and keep them on the second floor of their barns. They throw hay and grass up there for them to eat, and after a while they grow too big to come down so they just live their entire lives suspended off the earth by the barn's structure while they wait to be made into the family's dinner.

I climbed down the ladder bewildered from my morning cow kisses and was approached by a young man who spoke fluent English. He was a cousin of the family who had spent some time studying in the United States. He had been assigned to hang out with me and be my translator. He was excited about this task and was extremely proud of the fact that he could talk to the foreign girl. I was thankful to have someone who could explain the magic around me and bridge the gap between my new friends and me.

As we walked around I suddenly realized that we were so far out in the middle of nowhere, so far off the beaten path, that it was improbable that a white person had ever stepped foot in that village before, or if there had been, the times had been very few and far between. Everyone stared at me, and I was constantly surrounded by friendly children and women who just wanted to touch my hair and skin and be near me. I was used to this from Africa and was familiar with the attention. I had my translator ask the children all sorts of questions and to tell the women who asked me to be their best friend that "Yes, of course, I would love to."

I was shown the place where the huge wedding feast was being made and was surprised to see that all of the cooks were male. I was told that only Bramins, members of the cultural elite, could touch the food during preparation. They had white cloths tied around their waist and loins, and were making impossibly huge amounts of cooked food and salads.

I was then led to a group of women who were making bowls and plates out of banana leaves, using straw to hold them together. They were making hundreds of them, expecting everyone in the village to attend. This way, after the guests had their meal they could simply toss the bowl down to be dissolved back into the earth, and it was also free.

I helped them construct these clever little bowls until the wedding started, and then I followed the women to a small building. The bride was inside a dark room filled with candles, accepting wedding gifts from the villagers. One by one we walked up and gave her a gift. I placed some money in her palm, as it was all I had to offer, and then put a mixture of rice and wet red powder on her forehead as a bindi. By the time it was my turn to go, her forehead was totally covered with the thick red paste but I found a little exposed skin on the top and put my little bindi offering there. Then I looked down at the rest of her face and realized how young she was. I was told later that she was fifteen years old and had never spoken to the man who was to be her husband that afternoon. Their parents had arranged the marriage, and according to their custom, they had been allowed to look at each other once with the option for one of them to reject the other based on their looks, although this was more a formality rather than something that actually happened.

The young bride was led to a place outside where a group of women began to undress and wash her, then dress her again in bright red and gold-colored fabrics. They brushed and styled her hair, painted a small bindi on her forehead, which had been cleaned from the thick red paste, lavished her with attention and jewelry, and then took her to the wedding ceremony. The groom, on the other hand, had just arrived with his whole wedding party. He had been carried in a large cradle-type carriage by four strong men. They had walked for eight hours carrying the groom all the way from his house to hers, and I was told that he was not allowed to touch the ground in between. Everyone was singing and very excited. It turned out that the festive drumming and party sounds were coming from his village the night before. It is customary for the groom's family to celebrate the night before the wedding, as the groom does not leave the homestead, but rather brings home a new wife instead. They brought him to the place of the ceremony and he took his place next to the bride. He looked to be about eighteen years old and wore a navy suit, a tie and a pair of very gaudy fluorescent green plastic sunglasses.

The priest had created an intricate design of sacred geometric symbols on the ground with white flour, and placed offerings of flowers, food and drink to the gods on certain places on the design. He rocked back and forth as he sang the scriptures from a large book of holy sutras as he performed the ceremony in a language I couldn't understand, but it sounded very beautiful to my ears. Finally, he took the groom's hand and opened his palm and placed the bride's thumb inside of it. The groom wrapped his fingers around her thumb, and that was the sign that they were officially married.

The Bramins then served the delicious feast in the banana leaf bowls, and everyone ate and laughed and enjoyed the food and sunshine. After a few hours, the groom's wedding party picked up the bride and put her into the groom's carriage and carried her all the way back to his village. According to the custom, she also was not to touch the ground until she got there. While I thoroughly enjoyed the experience and privilege of attending this special Nepalese occasion, I couldn't help but feel sad for the young girl suddenly moved so far away from her family and felt my heart tug me in the direction of my own family back home. The difference being I was on my way back to my childhood home – and she was not.

I spent the remaining few days in Balaji's village going to the local school and teaching English to many different grades. The high school kids actually knew some English but the little kids knew none at all. I resorted to teaching them the names of body parts, like I did with the smaller children in Namibia. They laughed so much when I pointed to different areas on my face and repeated after me, "Noooozzze! Iiiiiiiizzze! Eeeeeearzzzzzz!" The part of me that thought I was finished with teaching was reminded that I did love it – especially the joy they brought into my own heart as they hungered for knowledge.

It was such a precious experience. I had a hard time saying my goodbyes. Balaji escorted me back to the nearest village where I could catch a bus; back down the rice paddies, across the river and through the fields. I eventually made my way back to the Annapurna circuit and spent my twenty-sixth birthday eating yak cheesecake with a German hiker and his Sherpa on that gorgeous trail, never in the least bit lost without a guide on that wide cobbled road.

I left Nepal with such a warm feeling in my heart, loving the beautiful people, their colorful, complex spirituality and culture, and headed to Thailand. I spent the Thai New Year at the largest water gun fight in the world in Chang Mai, rode elephants through the jungles, and bamboo rafts down beautiful streams, and took a day trip in a boat into Laos and Vietnam at the Golden Triangle. The spirit of adventure was alive in me and I loved this beautiful journey I was on. Then I made my way down to a gorgeous beach in the southern part of the country, where the blindness began…

The sisterhood I experienced in Ethiopia, the adventures of traveling with "Jesus," the lavishness of Italy, the wedding I witnessed in Nepal … These amazing memories brought up questions for me. Would I experience that kind of community and magic again? Would I be able to travel with a beautiful man by my side again? I loved my time in Italy, and saw what it was like to be blessed with material wealth, but at that time none of that was important to me. I wanted more chances, more life to live. And the wedding … Would I never have the chance to be married?

This is what you do when you are waiting to see if you will live or die. With a lot of time on my hands and so many fulfilling experiences to remember, I rode the wave of the highs and lows. I cherished my life with all my heart and longed for more.

Chapter 7

Dead Worm Party

The three weeks of taking the course of medication to kill the brain worms came to a close. Despite the weight gain and moodiness I felt well enough to continue on with my studies, albeit slowly. I had to take my finals late, but my mother went in with me to every exam. She sat with each professor telling him or her the entire story of the brain worms while I took the final. The professors never liked to give finals late, and most of them were a little suspicious as to why I needed to take it later than the other students, but each time I turned in my final, the professor, having just heard my saga from my dear mother, gave me a big hug and wished me well.

My mom returned to her home in Georgia, and I had peace and quiet at home once again. We weren't sure if the medication was effective yet, and I had to wait a few months before having a follow-up MRI to see if the tumors had shrunk. But I felt good. So, in the meantime, I was now on school break, the meds were done and I had time to rest.

One night I got a phone call from my mother's minister back in Georgia. He was the pastor of a Unity Church, the church she had started to attend while I was in the Peace Corps. I quite liked going to their church services when I visited my mama. They blended the teachings of Christ: love, forgiveness and compassion, with the teachings of the Buddha: presence, awareness and peacefulness, with the teachings of Native Americans and many other spiritual traditions. They were loving, open and kind, and I liked the minister that called. He conveyed his love and said he had been praying for me. He then offered to lead me through a meditation and I wholeheartedly said yes.

He asked me to sit quietly in my room and then led me through an experience I will never forget. I was asked to visualize myself in a beautiful landscape, one that gave me peace. He kept quiet for some time and allowed me to spend some time in this imaginary landscape. In my mind's eye I envisioned rolling green hills as far as the eye could see: vibrant, verdant hills with colorful flowers blooming here and there. The sky was peaceful, with soft billowy clouds painted across the blue expanse. There were trees in the distance but all around me were gentle hills with grass so soft it begged for bare feet to walk on it. I did just that. In my imaginary paradise I looked down and saw that I was stepping barefoot onto the velvety ground. The minister had me visualize a path in front of me, laid out for me. It led up a hill, and on the top of that hill was a bench. I sat down and just soaked up the peacefulness of this place for a while.

Then he told me that my guardian angel was approaching. He didn't describe my angel to me but my mind had constructed this beautiful woman: she had shiny light brown and blonde hair that fell in loose waves around her face. She was dressed in a soft yellow and green floral dress that clung slightly to her strong curves. She arrived at the bench and sat down with me. He gave me time to just be with her and have a long conversation. She said to me, "Everything is going to be alright. Everything that is happening is happening for a reason. You will understand that clearly in the future, but for now, be at peace. Know that everything is going to be fine."

After my guardian angel had said what she needed to say, she got up and walked back into the green hills, and somehow the minister knew just when to speak again. He now asked me to visualize myself rising from the bench and start walking down the path to go lead the rest of my life.

The meditation was over and I was flooded with peace. He told me that I could go back to visit that place, that bench, and my guardian angel at any time on my own. Over the years I did, and I am ever grateful for that gift. It was such good medicine for my soul.

When I returned to school the next quarter people didn't quite know what to say to me. I understood. I have been in their shoes when I have had friends and relatives diagnosed with cancer or some serious condition, and when you hear the news you don't know what to say or how to treat them. You try to act normal and not mention it too much, but you realize that it is the biggest thing they have ever had to face, and something that large would normally be something you would process with them and talk about. But you assume that they are tired of talking about it, of being it. So it becomes this huge elephant in the room that no one wants to talk about and that everyone pretends is not sitting there right in front of you. It pervades the air and all conversation even if it is not mentioned by name.

All of a sudden I was one of those people. Others found it hard to just hang out. They kept saying they were sorry and were a little stiff. You knew that when you walked away they would talk about it with the other people in the room. Not to mention I had ballooned in size and had zits covering me from head to toe as a result of the steroids. My self-esteem was dropping like a lead balloon and life became a little hard.

I found it very interesting that I had been so caught up with the world and its stresses before the seizure. Then when I thought I was going to die, all that old stress faded away and left me with a feeling of eternal spaciousness – an endless perspective that made all those menial problems seem meaningless. Then, when the correct diagnosis was made, treatment was given and I then stepped back into my "real life" again, that calm perspective went right out the window. All of a sudden I was concerned about the weight gain, zits, exams and paying my bills again. I suppose that is what real life is made up of, but I wanted to hold onto the lesson that superficial stuff isn't worth stressing over. That life is precious and can go at any time. But it was hard. I still got caught up in the little stuff.

The day finally came for me to go in for the follow-up MRI. It would be the telltale sign to see if the medication had worked or not. When the results were in, I went to the hospital with fear running through my body. The doctor sat me down and told me that the brain scans showed heat around some of the cysts, which indicated swelling but nothing that would pose a threat, she said. I would have to wait several more months to see if the drug cocktail really worked, but for now it all looked good. And I walked out of that appointment with hope. It seemed like I was going to be fine. And I breathed easier.

My doctor roommates and little brother threw a party for me to celebrate my recovery and the approaching end to the brain worm era. We made tons of nooses out of string that held gummy worms that we hung from the ceiling. A dead worm party! And yet it was actually a celebration of life, of health, of the medication being over – of the fear being over. It was a sweet celebration of love, and I sat in gratitude with my family and friends that night, smiling and hugging everyone and feeling thankful to be alive.

I headed back into schoolwork full force. I was accepted into a program called the Med-Advantage Program designed for students like myself who wanted to go to medical school. We got class credit for working in a local hospital that worked in partnership with the college. I shadowed doctors and worked in different areas of medicine. I worked in the emergency room first and witnessed little kids coming in with Q-tips stuck in their eardrums, watched a huge boil incised and drained, and even saw a man whose sleeve had gotten caught in a metal slicer which had pulled his forearm into the machine before the blades stopped. It was gnarly. That was all on the first day. I was also able to put on scrubs the following week and go in to observe a surgery. It was a fascinating experience.

The doctors that I worked with were all quite wonderful. I also worked with the physical and occupational therapists and found that I really liked this part of the healing process. In the post-operative rehab wing, we put people's knees into machines that moved their joints passively after they had gotten out of knee surgery, helped people learn to walk again, gave them exercises and helped them regain mobility. It was similar to the work I did in the Namibian hospitals. I definitely preferred the physical medicine to seeing arms eaten up by metal grinders or having to use scalpels.

It was during this time I realized that until that first seizure I had never been to a doctor before, yet I wanted to be one. I felt like as soon as it became clear that I wanted to become a healer and surrendered to that path fully, the universe said to me, "OK, girl. You are going to learn it from the patient's side of the table first." I learned first hand what it was like to lie in a hospital bed for days on end and have people come and put needles in you constantly. I learned what it was like to take medication after medication, hoping that your life didn't end. I had experienced how to find inner peace just in case your life was to suddenly end, and how to interact with people when they know you are sick with something serious. I started, during all those doctors' visits, doing my research: What was it like to be a patient in this person's hands? What kind of words did they use that made me feel better or worse? What did their office feel like and how would I have been more comfortable as a patient? What kind of philosophy did I have about healing in general?

Now that was the kicker. I hadn't thought about that too much before then. And, I was finding that I didn't really want to be the kind of "healer" that most of these doctors were. I had a different idea of what a positive healing atmosphere might feel like, rather than cold, white offices and hospital rooms with fluorescent lights and ugly posters. I had a different idea of what healing foods were besides the crap they served me in the hospital. I hadn't been able to put it into words quite yet, but this whole idea of holistic healing and how to be a healer was welling up in me as a result of my having experienced the patient's point of view.

One day while I was working in the hospital, I was talking with a doctor and was asking her if she loved what she did. She said, with some hesitation, "Yes, I enjoy it. But if I could do it all over again I would have gone to naturopathic medical school instead." I asked her what that was – I had never heard of a naturopath before. She gave me some websites to look up, and when I got home and pulled up the sites to the naturopathic medical schools, I was amazed. It was as if I was reading on the screen what had been forming in my head and heart but I hadn't been able to put into words quite yet. The idea of treating the cause instead of the symptoms, emphasizing prevention rather than dealing with the aftermath of poor health habits, and treating the whole person rather than just the parts as if they were not connected – all resonated with me deeply. Most importantly, I loved the philosophy that the body has an inherent ability to heal, and that medicine should be used to support and encourage the self-healing process. I was so moved by reading these philosophies that it turned my world upside down. I thought my path was clear about going to medical school. It was what I had been working towards and envisioned my path to be. But after exposure to a vitalistic philosophy that matched what was in my heart, I decided to apply to naturopathic medical school rather than the allopathic colleges.

Luckily, the prerequisites were exactly the same as for regular medical school, so I was on the right track already with the classes I was taking. I spent a long time filling out applications, writing essays and getting letters of recommendation together. After a couple months of waiting, I received letters from both colleges I applied to and was invited for interviews at both.

I bought a plane ticket to Portland, Oregon, rented a car and went to my first interview. I was so excited. It was my school of choice based on the schools' websites. The interview went well, but somehow I knew it was not the right choice for me. As a matter of fact, after spending the day at the school, I felt so deflated that I went to my friend's house that evening and got back on the internet to research other career options. The following morning I drove up to Seattle to an interview at the other school. I thought about not going, but when I drove onto that campus I could feel that it was a better choice for me. It felt right the whole way through. The school was nestled in a gorgeous forest, and I was in awe of the natural beauty of the campus grounds before I even reached the buildings. The interview went very well, and I was so relieved and excited. It seemed that I had found my place after all! I drove back to Portland, flew home and shared the news with my family and friends. I was set to start the following fall quarter.

A couple of weeks later I was driving home from the grocery store and I seemed to suddenly "wake up" in strange a way. I looked around and noticed that I had driven right past my apartment and was down the road quite a distance. I shook my head and wondered how I had managed to space out that completely. I turned around, parked and started walking the short block back to my apartment building.

Then, all of a sudden, the buildings started melting. The structures went from standing up straight and tall to curving in space and drooping over the road. I watched in confusion as the high rises looked like taffy being pulled and stretched. People started looking strange. My depth perception was totally off.

My whole reality started looking like a Salvador Dali painting.

I saw a strange man walk right up behind me. He stood an inch away by my right shoulder and looked at me out of the corner of his eyes. I quickly turned my head in fear of this creepy man looming over my shoulder, but when I looked, no one was there. He had disappeared. I saw creatures on the road intermingled with people. They looked like people but had strange looking appendages. When I looked straight at them to get a better look at these creatures they all of a sudden turned into real people again.

I wanted to get away, go home and escape from this terrible scene.

But I could not, for the life of me, remember where I lived.

Then I tried to think of what my name was, who I was.

And I didn't know.

Where was I even going?

Where was I?

Who was I?

I didn't know.

I didn't recognize anything.

I started to panic, but I didn't know where to go or what to do. There was not a single direction that looked normal.

After wandering the streets in this frightened state, things slowly started coming into focus. My breathing started to increase as panic set in. I started realizing that something had gone terribly wrong, that my perception had shifted, rather than the Dali painting–like "reality" being the real one.

At least I was able to make that distinction after a while.

And then I recognized the buildings around me. I had walked right past my apartment building, so I turned around and walked back to the front door. I entered into the elevator and looked at all the numbers on the panel but couldn't remember what floor I lived on and wasn't sure what button to push. A man got in the elevator with me and pushed a button on the panel. He looked towards the door that had still not closed. I told him that I felt really strange and that if I passed out he should call the hospital. He looked at me with suspicion and a little anger, asked me what drug I was on and left the elevator. I sat there for a few more seconds on my own, and then things started to come back to me. I remembered what floor I lived on. I pushed the button and the elevator door closed.

I finally made it down the hall to my apartment, and opened the door. I still felt very weird and began to get really tired.

I called 9-1-1.

When I arrived at the hospital, I was immediately put back onto an anti-seizure drug called Dilantin, which was the one that I had weaned myself off of a few months before. I didn't like taking drugs I didn't need, and I thought to myself that I would stop taking the anti-seizure medication and just carefully watch myself. Apparently that euphoric feeling I experienced before the grand mal seizure the previous year is called an aura and happens to some people before a seizure happens. I knew exactly what that felt like, so I made a deal with myself that I would watch myself carefully and if I felt an aura come on, or anything like it, or of course if I had another seizure, then I would take the drugs. But if I never had one again I didn't want to be taking the pills every day for no reason.

However, the doctors at the hospital explained to me that I was experiencing a different type of seizure that I didn't know about called a complex partial seizure. I was sent home from the hospital later that night with a prescription for Dilantin. The doctor also scolded me about my previous decision to wean myself off the drug. An emergency appointment was set up for the next morning with a neurologist.

I slept deeply that night.

The neurologist was the doctor I had worked with after my grand mal seizure, and I liked him. It was good to see a familiar face I could trust. He was pleasant, down-to-earth and was able to explain things to me in a way that made sense. He told me that the seizure I had the day before was due to the lesions in my brain. He suggested I get another MRI to see what was going on with the parasites at that point.

I was a little afraid to see what those scans would show.

I thought that the brain worm era was over!

I started to feel fear creep back into me, a heaviness crawl onto my back, and I didn't feel ready to deal with it all – *again*.

I went back to the doctor's office once a week to get my blood levels checked to make sure the Dilantin was being absorbed properly in my body.

Week after week I was told that my body was not absorbing the medication properly and then the neurologist would increase my prescription dosage. In the meantime, I kept experiencing similar hallucination periods during the complex partial seizures, in varying degrees.

Once I was jogging in a large park that I had run in many times in the past. I was on a flat trail that circumnavigated a beautiful lake. All of a sudden the trail started going up and down – and not only did I see the trail going up and down like little moguls, but I felt the hills inside my body as I jogged, seemingly going up and down.

However, at this point I had had so many of these seizures that I knew what they were. I was conscious of the fact that it was an abnormal sense of reality caused by my brain. When they came on I was able to separate the unreality my senses were registering from what I knew to be real. So the day I was jogging the imaginary moguls, somehow my brain remembered and registered that the path was really flat, that my brain was constructing something strange. And I knew it would all be over in just a matter of time so I tried to calm myself down, slow my breathing and just wait it out.

Even though sometimes I didn't know my name or where I was going, I was aware that it was a seizure of some sort and that it would soon be over if I could just be patient.

Weeks went by filled with weird seizures, and with each successive week they were less intense as my medication was increased – but they never ceased.

It was horrible.

My sense of reality shifted in and out of normal.

I once turned around in my apartment and my whole apartment was backwards. I gasped at first – it would always initially catch me by surprise, when I would turn my head and see things a different way, and my heart would stop for a second as I took in the strange sight – and then I would remember that it was a seizure.

I felt great fear – and totally ungrounded.

And I was always exhausted.

I went back for the scheduled brain MRI and the results were not good. It showed that the round of medication did absolutely nothing. The worms were still growing and putting pressure on different areas of my brain.

I have heard that your brain is the size of two fists put together. I looked down at my two fists and thought about what it was like in there, to have so many worms scattered throughout my brain.

It freaked me out.

The whole idea of having creatures in my brain was scary enough to begin with but now it was sinking in that these guys were there to stay and might end up wreaking havoc for a long while – or even kill me.

I just wanted to get them out.

I met with the infectious disease doctor who worked with me during the first round of medication. She explained that the whole drug cocktail I took before was experimental (she had explained that to me in the beginning too) and apparently I was one of the cases where it did not work. Since the medication had made me so ill and is a risky route to take to begin with, she suggested that I not try the cocktail again. Surgery was not worth the risk, considering the number of worms I had dispersed all over my brain.

The other route to take was to mask the seizures the best we could and wait out the life span of the worms. They were, she reminded me, not able to reproduce and would die within a few years.

A. Few. Years. What a mind trip.

After the sixth week of having partial complex seizures nearly every day, I was desperate to make everything stop. I was taking more than double the normal dose of Dilantin. I was having strange and terrible side effects and still the medication was not being absorbed into my blood properly for some reason.

The seizures were not nearly at the same magnitude but they still happened almost daily. Sometimes multiple times a day.

It got to a point that they became just a strange feeling in my body, especially when I exercised. Since I was a professional personal trainer and on my way to becoming a healer and teacher of health, exercise was a big part of my life. It took some time to realize that the seizures came on more often when I exercised, and when I realized that, I basically stopped exercising altogether. This made me feel even worse in other ways, as exercise was a great source of stress relief for me.

Finally, my doctor took me off the Dilantin and put me on another anti-seizure drug called Tegretol.

Miraculously, the seizures went away – immediately.

It was the magic pill for me.

My brain loved it for some reason, and I felt absolutely normal the day of the first dose. It was such a relief to live a day without having one of those episodes. Each day I had lived in terrible anticipation and scrupulous self-observation to see if another seizure would start, but while taking the Tegretol, they did not return.

I realized that I needed to find myself again and heal. A few weeks later I heard about an available room in an intentional community in north Denver, and it sounded like a good place to be.

The first time I heard about intentional communities was while I was traveling on a school break when serving in Namibia. I went to Tanzania with a friend and we took a ferry to the gorgeous, magical island of Zanzibar. I met two women there; beautiful, glowing women. One was the mother of a five-year-old boy (who wasn't with her at the time) and the other had been teaching art in Tanzania to deaf students. She had finished teaching and met with her friend to travel together for a while, and they were on their way back to Hawaii where they lived in an intentional community. They explained to me that this was a community where you had no belongings – whatsoever. When you moved in your money, debts, clothes, everything was given over to the community and shared. They had a small farm and grew all their own vegetables and home-schooled all the children who lived in the community. They lived quite naturally and sang, played music, worked outside and loved each other. She started telling me that they even shared lovers. There were no couples, per se, and they were all open with each other sexually. They explained that you would never have to do anything that you didn't want to do, but they all just loved each other very much, and they were all so healthy and glowing from their lifestyle that they were all naturally attracted to one another. And more importantly they all believed in sharing love and conscious sex freely. As a result, the women would get pregnant and usually not know who the father was. Once born, the child became part of the community's rather than your exclusive child. Everyone raised all the children.

The description of this place intrigued me greatly. I had never heard of anything like this before. I asked questions, which led to other questions. They were both so friendly and were totally willing to share details about their home life. Even after they left Zanzibar I still couldn't get them out of my mind, and the whole concept of that lifestyle and community opened me in a way – simply because I had never come across anything like it.

Later, when I was living with the two doctors in Denver before the grand mal seizure, I was playing on an Ultimate Frisbee team with them. I met a man on the team who asked me where I planned to move after my summer living at the doctors' home was up. I had thought about that quite a bit, actually, because I knew my time with the docs was coming to a close. I described to him my dream of finding an intentional community; a fantasy I had constructed in my mind after meeting those women. I loved the ideas but it was all too full on for my taste, and I envisioned something a little more balanced. I expressed that I wanted to live in an intentional community and share housing with people who lived as a family with unconditional love and support for one another. I wanted to share household chores, space, meals, but no more. I needed my money to be separate and I certainly didn't want to have sex with my housemates. I dreamed of a shared garden, a hot tub and pets.

As I spoke, his jaw dropped. He said he just happened to live in such a community. I did not believe him at first but he invited me over to see for myself. The following week when I arrived, I shook my head in amazement. He was telling the truth. This was exactly what I had described to him. I was impressed at what they had created. Years prior, four people had gotten together and bought two homes next door to each other. They tore down the fence that divided the two homes and started a huge garden on the shared land. They built a fire pit and put a hot tub in the yard. The community had grown to seven people, plus a dog and two cats. The residents each had a night when they would cook for the rest, and they shared meals together if they happened to be home. There were bimonthly house meetings when they spoke of any mundane house stuff – bills and the like, and they also used this time to check in with each other to see if anyone needed some support, hugs, love or help.

They just happened to have a room available and I was excited to move in.

I loved it from the start.

The people were all about my age, maybe a little older. I was surprised and delighted by their integrity, maturity and joyfulness. It was such a healing environment for me. It was biking distance from my college; the hot tub helped melt my built-up tension; the new friendships were uplifting and positive and it was just a good place for me to be. I had two quarters left of school and the seizures seemed to be gone. It felt like I was given a new start.

Two months after moving in I met a man who went by the name of Jayden. He had an identical twin brother that looked and sounded so much like him, even their own mother could not tell them apart. I was told she had to part their hair on different sides when they were younger to know who was who. And yes, they did part their hair on the opposite sides sometimes just to get away with much naughtiness.

He was amazing. He was a pure ball of love and free energy, quite unlike anyone I had ever met. We fell in love immediately and spent as much time together as possible. However, he lived in San Francisco, so we were flying back and forth every two to three weeks to see each other. I had a personal training client who flew all the time for work and did not want to leave his family to fly anywhere else when he had any time off, so we traded sessions for frequent flier miles, and every few weeks I had a romantic weekend on the West Coast with my new love.

As December and my graduation approached, we decided to move in together. I took my last final and moved across the country for true love.

Chapter 8

Golden Gateway

I flew to San Francisco and was picked up by Jayden himself. We were both so excited. It was a bold step to move across the country just for a chance at love, and I was all in. I moved into his house, and before too long had become good friends with his roommates and started looking for a job. About two weeks later I landed a wonderful job working for a physical therapist managing two wellness centers that were focused on back strengthening and rehabilitation. It paid well, was biking distance from the house, and promised opportunities for me to both learn and grow. The job was due to start in a few weeks time.

At that point I was due for a follow-up MRI of my brain just to make sure things were coming along well with the Cerebral Cysticercosis. I expected the scans to show that the lesions were shrinking and that everything was going away at that point.

But the results were not good at all. As a matter of fact, they were alarming and very confusing.

They found three new cysts in my brain that were not on the initial scans – and all the existing ones were still growing.

The presentation of the new worms caused the doctors to believe that I had a mother worm living in my gut after all. The little guys in my brain were not able to reproduce and I was obviously not exposed to new worms since I had returned from Africa, so they were afraid that the new ones must have come from a long worm living in my gut laying eggs, meaning that I was self-infecting. I had been repeatedly tested for one of those lengthy worms living in my intestines when I had my first seizure, and each time the tests were negative. However, they were now convinced that the worm must have been embedded in the mucous lining of my intestines and had escaped the previous tests.

I was scared to death.

Again, I thought this journey had come to a close.

I was ready to start this wonderful next stage of my life and be done!

But there I was still deep in it and getting more bad news.

The doctors gave me some medication to strip the mucous lining of my intestines and I did another stool test. Yet even after all of that – the test results were negative again.

I did not have a mama worm in my intestines.

They were puzzled about that, but even more so they were concerned as to what our next plan of action would be to deal with the growing number of worms in my brain.

I had again taken myself off the anti-seizure medication a few months prior and had made the decision to watch myself closely for auras or complex partial seizures. And I had had so much experience at that point with the hallucinatory seizures that I was able to remain calm even throughout the altered state of consciousness. And so it was. I watched myself, constantly examining any strange sensation that came over me. I was waiting for a seizure – and waiting even longer for those little buggers to die.

The doctors came to the same conclusion as before, that I should not try the drug cocktail again, that surgery was not a good option for me, and that I should just wait out the lifespan of the worms and mask the symptoms as they appeared.

In the mean time, there I was in a new city far from my friends and family. My job hadn't started yet and I just heard the news about the cysts.

I started to feel a dark cloud come over me.

I had never felt it before, and it felt endless and empty like a void of hopelessness.

It came and went at first, and then it became heavier and harder to ignore. It got to the point that sometimes I couldn't go out of the house, and eventually I felt extreme pain if anyone saw me so I hid out in my room. Mostly under the covers.

Before I knew it, I was knocked out.

The depression hit me so hard that I spent several days under the covers. I begged my boyfriend not to leave me alone, but he just didn't know what to do. His super high-energy natural state was so out of sync with what was the lowest energy of my life, and he couldn't help but feel that he just didn't know me. Whenever he left me in the room alone for any length of time at all, I felt totally abandoned and would spend the day endlessly contemplating suicide.

I was so hopeless and tired that I didn't even want to get better. I felt so, so exhausted – physically, yes, but more on a soul level. I can't explain how incredibly and painfully tired I felt.

It just didn't feel human.

It felt like I could not possibly be that tired from any life experience that exists. And the seconds seemed like days, and the days seemed like painful lifetimes.

It felt like an infinite chasm of darkness and emptiness that sucked my soul away. I couldn't take it any more.

It hurt just to be alive.

It hurt to be awake.

I wanted to sleep, and if I couldn't sleep I wanted to die.

I thought about hurling myself off the Golden Gate Bridge, and I sat and imagined it all day long, over and over again, there under the dark covers. But I did not have the energy to even make it out of the room.

So my death occurred in my mind only – again and again.

Several days later – or maybe a week? Maybe two? I don't know how much time passed during that dark night of the soul. But one day, light started appearing at the end of the tunnel. Just the fact that it was there gave me more energy. I could face the chance of running into a room-mate in order to get a meal or use the bathroom, and I finally opened the blinds a little to let some sunlight in, literally and figuratively. I began to go on walks. And I started to feel like myself again. The curtain lifted just as mysteriously as it had come, and just in time for my new job to begin. I was lucky that the program I was working with was just starting so my work hours were light, and steadily increased with time, as did my energy.

Shortly afterwards I had my twenty-eighth birthday, and Jayden gift-ed me a wonderful massage, the first professional massage of my life.

It was heavenly.

We went home and a friend called me to wish me a happy birthday. As I laid on the bed talking on the phone, Jayden looked at me and came to the realization that he didn't really know me, that he loved someone that he thought was me, and that this woman sitting on his bed talking to a friend, this woman who had just exhibited such crazy emotional be-havior, was not the woman he loved. He explained all this after I hung up, and this news sent me spiraling again into depression.

I have to give credit to this man, who fell in love with me, carried on a long-distant relationship, giving a big "yes" to trying it all out. He saw my best side, and then my worst side as soon as I moved into his bedroom.

I did not blame him.

I didn't know how to handle what was going on with me either, or know why it was happening. The whole experience took us both on a crazy ride, and he was tired and didn't want to do it any more. Understandably so.

But I felt abandoned and unwanted. And I was far from my friends and family. I cried and cried myself into exhaustion that night, and I felt my body contract and become so sour that I remembered thinking to myself, "Wow, I need a massage," when ironically, I had just received one that very afternoon.

It was not a good birthday after all.

I quickly found a new home close to my job, and as time went on I developed a thick skin. Although I wasn't feeling great inside, I found the strength to keep going, to show up at work and smile and do what I needed to do, yet when I went home and was alone, I cried and questioned and felt my heart twist into a knot at night. But the days kept going on – and so did I.

And thus began my solo journey exploring San Francisco.

A few weeks later I met a hip, young photographer who had lived in the city for a long time and had been involved with many different communities over the years. He asked me what I was into and what I was looking for at that time in my life. I told him that I loved to dance, that I was very spiritual though no longer followed any certain religion and that I needed healing, so if I could find a community that combined those things, I would be delighted. He knew of such a community and said they were having a dance celebration to honor the spring equinox. He arranged for me to pick up an invitation at the end of the week and I went to this sweet event.

And this night ended up changing my life.

The celebration was held in a century-old neo-Gothic church in the heart of the Mission District of San Francisco. It was not a Christian group but had somehow worked it out with a liberal church to hold their celebrations in this church. I found out later that about one hundred people had worked to put this event together, doing everything from decorating the entire church, including the bathrooms, to organizing volunteers whose only job was to give you a huge hug when you walked in the door to welcome you. There were about three hundred and fifty people there of all ages, including children and people in their sixties. The environment felt mature, beautiful, open and free. It was such a sacred experience dancing in a place of worship, because that is how I felt when I danced – sacred. I had been to nightclubs and knew that dance felt right for my body but the nightclub environment felt so unhealthy.

This was different. There was a freedom there for me to move my body as it wanted to be moved. Hour upon hour I danced and sweat poured from me. It was as if I spoke in tongues like I did back when I was in the church, but it was through movement of my body instead of with my vocal cords. I was a conduit for Spirit to flow through me, through my body, through uninhibited movement. I felt as if there was no separation between God and me, which was a shift from my earlier beliefs, because according to the Christian doctrine I had wholeheartedly embraced as a youth, I was here on Earth and God was up in the Heavens somewhere, definitely distinct from me. I could pray to Him but it was like I was on the phone with Him, not at one with Him.

Dancing in that church I felt at one with Spirit, the universe, even the people I was dancing with, because I really got it on a soul level that they, too, were at one with Spirit and we were one in the dance. Just pieces of the same spirit energy dancing with itself that had manifested differently in each person, with different colored hair and different movements. We celebrated that radiant spirit in each of us and gave gratitude with our hands up in the air as we danced through the large beautiful space.

I met so many wonderful people that night, forming friendships that would end up lasting years and years, perhaps for the rest of my life. I became actively involved with the community after that lovely night. I went to the monthly meetings that addressed the business matters of the group, went to the choir concerts they had which embraced poetry and music from all spiritual traditions or none at all, got invited to all the birthday parties, housewarming parties, dinner parties, small get-togethers and dinners. After a while I was just one of the clan and I started to brighten up from that deep dark depression I had fallen into upon landing in San Francisco.

I was still on my path to begin naturopathic medical school in Seattle. Although I had landed a good job in the field of healing, my path was calling me to be and do more than that. I was scheduled to start classes that fall. I had worked hard to get to that point. And yet although I was doing better, I was still sick. I was emotionally unstable and there was no way I would be able to thrive in a stressful, demanding program like that. The thought came to me that I needed to defer my enrollment.

I felt totally deflated.

I wanted so badly to get on with my life and work towards my goals. But I was not in a place to do that. I called the school and explained I was not well and needed to defer my start date. They put my file on hold and said I could begin the following year.

In the meantime, I decided to check out naturopathy as a patient for the first time. I started to see a naturopathic doctor, who was also an acupuncturist, to treat my depression and the Cerebral Cysticercosis. The treatments helped me in some ways but not in others. The stripping of the mucous lining of my gut that I had experienced months before left me feeling weak and my digestion was off for quite a while after that. After seeing the naturopathic doctor and taking the herbs he prescribed, I started feeling more balanced, like my inner fire was returning. My digestion was better and my mood was improving, but it didn't feel that it was really enough to make me feel "normal" again, especially emotionally. After a while, I could not afford the treatments anymore and I had to stop going.

At the end of the year my boss told me that he was leaving his physical therapy practice and wanted to manage the wellness center full-time, which was my job. Thus, due to this reorganization I was let go.

Just like that.

He said I was doing a great job and that he would give me a great recommendation for another job, but I was no longer needed.

The bleakest part of winter slowly passed, mirroring my inner darkness.

I tried to pull myself up by my own bootstraps. By January I had landed a job as a personal trainer in a top-of-the-line gym in downtown San Francisco, and had finished the massage therapy training I had been attending on weekends and evenings for the last year. I started out well in the personal training job, and had a massage therapy practice on the side, out of my home.

But as the months went by, I started having crazy amounts of anxiety – at first every week or so and then daily. I experienced an overwhelming feeling that would totally envelop me. It felt as though something was dreadfully wrong, as if someone had just told me that my entire family had just died, but when I searched myself for why I was feeling such anxiety and dread, I couldn't come up with any answer. Truly.

There was nothing there to cause these feelings, but they were there, unavoidable. I could not ignore them and at times they were incapacitating. Fear would grip my belly and I would have an incredible amount of energy course through my chest until it was spreading throughout my body.

I sometimes had to cancel all my clients and just sit with this fear, this terrible feeling. I would sit in meditation and try in vain to figure out the cause of these feelings. I never came up with anything, though. Money was a little tight, but not that bad, and canceling my clients just made that situation worse, so I didn't feel like that could have been the cause. I had made it with much less income than that before. Yet I was becoming unreliable and canceled too often as the months wore on. I lost some clients over it, and before long I had hardly any income at all.

By the end of the year I was having full-on panic attacks.

I would start shaking and getting so nervous and worked-up that I started hyperventilating. It was kind of like having a seizure in a way.

Then they started happening more often, even while I was at work. It was freaking people out, including myself, and it got to the point that I was truly unable to live a normal life at all.

No insurance company would accept me for health coverage with the horrendous medical history I had under my belt. I was denied coverage by every plan I applied to because I had a pre-existing condition: the Cerebral Cysticercosis. And I could not afford to go to a doctor and pay out of pocket. But eventually I was so desperate for help I did what I had to do. I found a free clinic in San Francisco and checked myself in to get seen by a professional. Unfortunately, I ended up sitting in the waiting room for hours upon hours. The clinic worked on a triage system and the most emergency-based patients were seen first. I saw people coming in with all sorts of conditions, seemingly drugged out of their mind or cut to pieces from a gang fight. The weepy girl in the corner didn't pose a threat nor seem to be in a state that needed urgent care. So there I was in a dirty, urine-smelling and depressing waiting room in downtown San Francisco, sitting next to crack dealers and prostitutes, wondering how my life had come to this.

I felt dejected, shameful and desperate. Wasn't I supposed to be a doctor by now? Wasn't I well-educated and on my way to success? And yet I was broke, sitting in a disgusting clinic surrounded by what some would call the dregs of society. And I was one of them.

Finally, at the end of the workday they led me in to see a counselor. This man asked me about my medical history and my symptoms and immediately suggested that I see an infectious disease doctor, as he thought that the panic attacks were due to the Cerebral Cysticercosis.

I was flabbergasted. I had been watching myself so closely making sure that I didn't have another grand mal seizure or bout of hallucinatory seizures. But I was never told to be on the lookout for depression or anxiety, that these might be symptoms caused by the brain parasite.

But shortly after that, when I met with the team of infectious disease doctors at Stanford University Hospital, paid for by Worker's Compensation because I had contracted the parasite while an employee of the U.S. Peace Corps, they explained that it was common to experience emotional imbalances after seizures. One doctor told me that seventy to eighty-five percent of the people who experience seizures at the magnitude that I did later experience symptoms of depression, bipolar disorder or anxiety.

I wish I had known that before. So much of my suffering would have made sense to me.

They also explained why the three cysts that looked new on the previous MRI scans were there. They did not think I had been infected again, or that they were new at all, but said that an MRI of a brain with tumors in it is like a slicing a loaf of bread with M&M's in it. It is possible for the M&M's to be inside the slice of bread, hence not show up on a scan. But if the M&M's were to grow, then it would become visible after a while. We also spoke about the possibility of another round of treatment to kill the worms, but like before, decided that the toll on my body wasn't worth the try. The best bet would be to mask the symptom — and instead of it being seizures this time it was the anxiety and depression. They suggested that I see a psychiatrist.

I was so relieved to have an answer, to understand why I was going through such crazy bouts of dark depression, anxiety and later the panic attacks. I had questioned myself so much during those times. I believed all those negative voices in my head when I felt that life wasn't worth living, or that there was something terribly wrong yet I couldn't figure out what it was.

I never questioned that those feelings were there because of abnormal activity in my brain *due to the worms.*

I had to put in my notice to quit my job at that point, as I only had a few clients left anyway and the amount of stress it put on me to make the scheduled meetings was too much. Funny how something that seems so normal at one time can be so heavy a burden at another.

I started seeing a psychiatrist at Stanford who was supportive of me wanting to use alternative medicine to deal with my symptoms, rather than go the allopathic medicine route right away. I met with him every few weeks at first and then every six weeks or so. But our meetings were only fifteen minutes long or less. It was hard to explain what was going on in such a short amount of time. And although I couldn't really afford it, I started seeing acupuncturists and naturopathic doctors that worked on a sliding fee scale to try to treat it with natural medicine instead.

I tried everything I could to deal with the anxiety. And yet none of this was working to stop the emotional roller coaster.

I started falling into another depression as well.

I was watching my life fall apart again and didn't feel like I could hold on to the slippery slope to pull myself up and out of this soupy mess.

I had a lot of time on my hands, and yet when things were quiet and I was alone I was so very scared and depressed. I tried to distract my-self constantly by seeing friends, going to movies, reading stories about people who lived in distant lands – anything to keep my mind off of the tumors in my brain and the effects they were having on my life.

One night when I was going to a movie by myself, I felt like I hit a wall. I actually felt something hit my chest and I "woke up." I realized that I was diverting my attention away from my fears. I knew it needed to stop, and that I needed to face and integrate what was going on with me.

I turned my car around and drove home, parked and went up to my room. I sat down in meditation, and without the intention of it happen-ing, a vision came before me. Some people visualize things when they meditate. I usually did not. I focused on my breath, on the sensations in my body, on being awake to what was around me and inside of me. But this evening it was as if a movie was playing before my very eyes. I didn't know where it came from but it was clear and powerful.

I saw myself walking, struggling to move forward, but it was such a chore and I wasn't moving very fast despite my efforts.

I then noticed that there were ropes coming off of my back, leading down to a large box that was dragging on the ground behind me. These ropes were not tied around me but seemed to meld right into my skin, made out of my own body's material. They were part of me and were attached to this box on the ground, which was incredibly heavy. No matter how hard I tried to keep walking forward and away from the box I kept dragging it along and never gained any distance from it. It was slowing me down and it took quite a bit of effort just to walk ahead. I knew somehow that the box contained all my fears. Fears that I had never faced, fears that didn't have a name. But I could see plainly that I had to go back to that box and face it all or it would be dragging behind me, holding me back for the rest of my life.

I had to turn around and open it, peer inside and face the demons I had grown inside this container. I gathered up all the courage and strength I had, and walked back to the box on the ground. Although I was watching this all happening as if it was a movie, I could feel the fear inside of me fully. I could also feel the courage that I gathered. It filled my body and gave me the strength I needed. I took hold of the flaps of the box and pulled them apart, quickly and fiercely, ready to face the ugliness of my dark world.

But instead of unbearable fears to face, the box immediately disintegrated to dust on the floor. The whole box started to blow away in the wind as tiny particles of dust. There was nothing inside.

There were no fears and there was no box.

There was nothing.

The whole thing was just an illusion.

All I had to do was look inside of it for it to disappear.

Then a voice spoke clearly and said to me: "Everything that is happening is happening for a reason. Layers are being peeled away and a healer is being born from within. And her name is Ashanna."

Then the whole vision disappeared and it was quiet.

All of a sudden I was back in my room sitting on the floor.

Changed forever.

Blessed with a teaching I needed desperately, blessed with a new name: Ashanna. I was born on 3-7-73, and my mother named me Shannon

Kellie. She often called me Shan, but I had never heard the name Ashanna before. It was interesting to me how Ashanna was similar to Shannon, or Shan, how the new name had my old name embedded in it. But it was definitely a new name altogether.

At first I said the name over and over.

I kept this vision and this name to myself for several days, going over it in my mind and heart a million times.

A few days later, the spiritual dance community I had been part of had a gathering to honor the winter solstice. I asked a few friends there to call me Ashanna instead of Shannon. It was a powerful thing for me to take on, and the new name had a very different energy when people said it. I had never even thought of changing my name before, and it was not a conscious choice when that voice spoke to me, but it was perfect for me to do at that time, as it turned out. A few weeks later I wrote a long email telling everyone in my life about my vision and name change and took the name on fully.

Chapter 9

Walking the Good Red Road

I was seeing a naturopath several times a week. I took vitamins and herbs and received acupuncture two or three times a week for the anxiety. I started an intense cleanse that was absolutely amazing for me. It was the first major cleanse I had ever done and the effects were quite profound. However once I finished cleansing, my eating habits went back to the way they were, and the glow and peace I had during the detox started to fade.

I started going to therapy as well, trying to express with words what was happening in my life. It was the first time I had seen a counselor on a regular basis, and it was a wonderful healing tool for me.

During this time I met a very special man. He was a Native American healer, a medicine man that ran traditional pipe ceremonies out of his house once a week. His name was Nathaniel. During his pipe ceremonies he packed his pipe with herbs – not tobacco, marijuana, or anything addictive or hallucinogenic – and passed around the pipe. The people in the circle would put their prayers into the pipe and pass it on, and then we smoked the pipe, each person either taking a puff or holding the pipe to our hearts if we didn't want to inhale, letting the smoke rise to the gods and our ancestors to see and read and answer. He also spoke before and after he passed the pipe, sharing spiritual teachings that were synthesized from the Lakota Indian tradition, as well as Buddhist, Taoist, Christian and other teachings. His messages felt right in my heart and I loved the ancient ceremony he offered. He ran his ceremonies in a very particular way, adhering to the ancient ways of the Lakota Indian people, and his teachings were grounding, centered on love and were very matter-of-fact. I cherished praying in a group, supporting others in their prayers, sitting in meditation and receiving teaching and love from this extraordinary man.

I had an idea brewing in my head for a long time of going on a vision quest. I didn't know much about them but the thought kept coming back to me over and over throughout the years. It occurred to me that he might lead them and so I asked him one day if he ever facilitated vision quests. He lit up and said he had been praying for the opportunity to do one but needed some help and the right land to run it on. I happened to know some older women who lived in the forest of Santa Cruz who rented out large yurts on their property for small groups. The land surrounding the yurts was theirs too, and was gorgeous – sacred. I felt like it was the right place. I asked the women if they would be OK with us doing a vision quest ceremony there and they were delighted to host it. I took the medicine man to the land and he felt it was the right place as soon as he stepped out of the car – an answered prayer. There was a perfect spot for a sweat lodge down by a stream, complete with stacks of wood for the fire and lots of space in the fields for the participants to spend their time in solitude during the quest.

And so I became Nathaniel's assistant and we started planning a vision quest. We told everyone who attended the pipe ceremonies about the quest and all the available spots filled immediately. I went to work finding the things we needed for the ceremony. Nathaniel instructed me that whenever I did work on this project I had to do it "in a good way." I had to center myself in my heart and do everything with conscious awareness. Even if I were to buy a bucket, I had to buy it from a person who had good energy. If the person selling the bucket was exuding bad energy, I was instructed to pay more down the street from a kind, smiling person rather than buy the cheaper one from the negative person. If I was feeling negative myself or down, I couldn't work on the project. Only when I had love in my heart was I allowed to do the work. I practiced this every time I worked on this project, and eventually found that this amazing way of being began to permeate into the rest of my life. I started to feel this huge lesson of truth seep into my soul.

Finally the weekend for the vision quest ceremony arrived. The group of twenty people met on the land and we began to build the sweat lodge from scratch. We cut down tree saplings that the older women had marked for us to use, which also helped them keep their land healthy. We collected the young trees and used special tools to strip the bark off of them, leaving the cut trees supple and flexible. We bent them to shape the lodge and secured the whole thing with twine, then covered the lodge with tarps, sheets and blankets. We worked mostly in silence with a reverence for the process that was occurring.

There was a man who had volunteered to be our fire keeper throughout the ceremony. He had been tending a large fire since early that morning and his job was to constantly watch the fire and keep it at the proper size and temperature all day and night until the end of our ceremony. His care for the fire was shining from within him in a gentle but solid way and he was on task with loving attention to the flame.

We followed the medicine man's instructions about how to walk around the fire and lodge only in a certain direction, and we built an altar on a mound of dirt with special items people had brought, including the pipe that Nathaniel usually used in our prayer circles. Finally we were ready to enter the lodge and to cry out for a vision. We all piled into the lodge, crawling through the tiny door on our hands and knees in the dirt, circling the center of the lodge in a clockwise direction to take our seat. We sat in complete darkness, huddled around the center as the volcanic rocks from the fire were brought in one by one while the medicine man chanted and sprinkled cedar and other things on the glowing rocks.

It got warmer with each rock that arrived and eventually it seemed so hot I didn't think I could take it any more. But more rocks came. I was pushed beyond my limits with the heat and the steam as they poured water over the rocks. The medicine man knew, though. He knew we were safe and he was taking care of us.

We all sat in complete trust.

Normally a sweat lodge is four rounds. He explained that the four rounds could never be changed or broken except in the case of the vision quest. It was a time when only two rounds were done, and then the people came out of the lodge to go cry for a vision. After the quest in the forest was over, we were to return to the lodge to finish the last two rounds and then the ceremony was complete. According to tradition, since we were to be fasting during the whole vision quest, after the last round in the sweat lodge we were to share a huge meal that had been prepared by volunteers there to support us. While we were suffering the heat during the first two rounds in the lodge, we all took turns praying that we all do this quest in a good way, to be strong and for us to get exactly what we needed. Between all the songs we sang, listening to the teachings shared by Nathaniel and remaining attentive to the twenty people saying their sincere prayers, it seemed like we were in there forever.

When I didn't think we could take the heat any more, magically, the medicine man told the fire keeper to open the door and we left the lodge. We walked slowly in meditation across the bridge over the stream, through the trails in the forest to the opening that revealed a giant field. In silence, we all went our separate ways to find the place that was to be our own private circle to have our quest, and we then laid out the prayer ties we had made.

In the weeks prior to the sweat lodge ceremony, the medicine man instructed us all to make over 400 prayer ties. To make a prayer tie you had to cut red material into a small square a couple of inches wide and deep. We took pinches of tobacco and infused each one with a heartfelt prayer. We put the tobacco in the middle of the swatch of cloth, folded it in a particular way that held the tobacco inside, then tied the swatch together with string so the tobacco was secured in a little tiny bundle on one end with the extra cloth at the other, so it looked like a little present. We each strung over 400 bundles together and had these long ropes of our tobacco-bundled-prayers with us when we arrived in the field. When we found our individual places to have our vision quest, we laid out the prayer ties in a circle that enclosed our personal space. We did not venture beyond the borders of our prayer tie halo and spent over twenty-four hours encircled and held by our invocations, with nothing but some water, our journal, a blanket and our prayers.

I was expecting this experience to be very difficult for me. I was concerned about the fasting, the elements, and long hours with no distractions, but when I crested the hill and looked down I saw a huge grandmother tree that looked over the entire field. I knew that my spot was under her branches. I walked through the tall grass right to a flat spot in the shade, with some sunlight coming through the tree for warmth but with the shelter of the leaves when I needed respite from the bright rays. The weather was beautiful, as if the earth was happy we were doing this and cooperated fully to make it a pleasurable experience for us. The wind was blowing slightly and the sun was warm but not hot. There were a few billowy clouds in the sky but no threat of rain, only gorgeous shapes to watch dance along as the day passed by.

I laid out my prayer tie circle and put my blanket in the center and drank some water, as I was thirsty after sweating so much in the lodge. I spent the day on my back and was visited periodically by a mouse; a super cute, fluffy little mouse that came by as if to say hello, and check me out curiously but not bother me. I was grateful for this little creature's friendship and periodic visits. And yet in the expanse of time between the mouse medicine, I was open – open to a message. I was crying for a vision for my life, a sense of purpose. I wanted, with desperation, some sort of explanation as to why I never seemed to be able to continue on my path as a healer because my health was never stable long enough for me to return to school and actually qualify in some sort of healing art. I asked for an explanation for the brain tumors. I questioned God why all this was happening to me. I felt I was being punished. I had gone to the African bush to serve people, to live selflessly and was rewarded with this horrendous disease, a disease that was not well known to doctors, difficult to treat and caused all sorts of weird symptoms. At times I wished for the disease to be more concrete, that my arms or legs had fallen off. At least people could see that and understand it, could actually know how the disease was affecting my life. But instead I looked fine on the outside with my insides suffering from an insidious all-pervasive sickness that kept me from leading a normal life – a heavy burden to bear.

I sat with my prayers crying for clarity. Then after all this crying, all this praying for an explanation, a voice came to me and said very simply:

"Have faith. And when you don't have faith, pray for faith."

And then there was silence.

In that moment I felt in touch with infinite space around me, connected to all things. And I had a knowing that this was the answer to my prayers.

Not a message I would have wished for, as it seemed like a vague answer to my questions, but the perfect answer. So I wrote those words in my journal and watched the sun go down. I wasn't sure if I was going to sleep there on that vision quest, but I had such a peace come over me, like my hard work was finally finished and that now was the time to be truly peaceful – such a special gift to me.

I had my answer.

Wrapped in my blanket, I then drifted off to sleep with peace in my heart and woke later to the first light of dawn.

I watched the sky change colors and listened as the birds and animals awoke and began to sing and rummage around. Before I knew it, the sound of the drums back at the fire began drifting loudly over the treetops. People were singing, chanting and calling us back to the sweat lodge to complete the last two rounds. The vision quest participants seemed to come out of nowhere as we all gathered our belongings and converged back into the main field, ready to walk the trail back over the bridge. We acknowledged each other with a nod, yet walked in total silence back to the lodge and crawled in that little door into the darkness once more.

We repeated the ritual of having the volcanic rocks brought in, one by one, as the medicine man sprinkled cedar on them. The door was closed, and with so many hot rocks and all of our bodies in that small space the heat seemed unbearable, and we were all light-headed from not having food for over a day. But we did it. We all prayed again, thanking Spirit for the guidance and the teachings. We then had another round in which more stones were brought in and we chanted in the dark, digging our fingers into the cool dirt, searching for some sort of respite from the heat. We were crying, sweating, hungry, empty yet full, shining and radiant, even in our weakness.

The door was opened for the last time, and we crawled out one by one in the dirt to lie down on the ground to drink some water. When we had the strength, we walked up to the yurts for a shower before we shared a gorgeous family feast. We talked about our experiences with excitement, the food and showers having given us a renewed abundance of energy. Some people had expected it to be hard, like myself, but had actually had an easy time of it. Some thought it would be easy, but they had the hardest time. Others had no expectations at all and had varying degrees of struggle and peace. All of us had such different experiences. It was fascinating, but no doubt a beautiful and powerful experience for all of us.

Summer went by and before I knew it autumn was upon me. I continued to go for regular appointments for the anxiety and intermittent depression. The natural remedies were working somewhat, but not enough to really do the trick. I continued to swim in a darkness that seemed too slippery to climb out of. I had to defer my education yet again, and after I called the school to let them know I could not come, I started to cry.

I walked back to my room, collapsed on the floor and cried for a long time. The house was empty so I was able to cry loudly if I had wanted to, but instead I felt so twisted inside, and I rolled and writhed on the floor asking "Why?" in a voice so quiet it was almost inaudible. My face was contorted with grief and suffering.

Again those familiar feelings came. Feelings of victimhood.

I felt like I was continually being punished.

And for what?

I did not know.

By whom? God?

So I started asking God, quietly, then louder and louder with each minute.

"Why? Why are you doing this to me? What did I ever do? Why is this happening?"

Then anger rose up in me and I got in touch with rage. A desperate rage that wanted answers. "Why?" I screamed.

I don't know how long I stayed on the floor but the release of pent up emotion felt beneficial. Then I remembered the words that were in my journal from my vision quest: "Have faith. When you don't have faith, pray for faith."

I did my best to offer up the smallest prayer for faith, for in that moment I had none at all. It was not a sweet prayer "Dear God, please give me faith." It was "Fuck you. If faith is what I need then give me some – 'cause I am all out!"

By the time the autumn leaves turned golden red something else started to happen. I wasn't sure if it was an answered prayer or just the natural progression of the roller coaster ride I was on – but I started to feel something different.

An energy started flowing through me.

I still didn't feel well and I couldn't handle being around too many people, but I felt like I was connected to Spirit in a way that I had never experienced before.

I started channeling messages for myself and for other people.

One woman told me she thought I was psychic. She went and got her boyfriend and other friends and brought them over to my house for me to "channel" for them. I had messages in words and pictures come to me and I shared everything that was given to me. It always made sense to the people receiving it, even when it didn't make sense to me, and they left amazed and very grateful.

After a few weeks I felt like I was receiving a clear message: *I had everything that I needed and should give away all my belongings and go to Hawaii.*

I know it sounds kind of crazy, but at the time the calling was very clear and I was living on a higher plane of reality – so I thought. I didn't even question it. I didn't know what was waiting for me in Hawaii but I had heard from many people over the years about a certain valley on the island of Kauai that was, for lack of a better word, "calling" to me. Some people said that Rainbow Children lived there. I wasn't even sure what that meant, but I had a fascination with that place ever since I heard of it, and now it felt like I was supposed to go there.

So I did just that. I sent out an email to all my friends and said, "Come and get it. I am moving away and I am giving away all my belongings." I even gave away my car. I left with a large backpack, very little money, no plan and didn't know when I was going to return.

I landed on the island of Kauai and hitchhiked up to the northern part of the island where a friend had a beautiful house that I could stay in for a few days before I went into the wilderness. He lived in California so I had the whole place to myself. It was gorgeous, complete with manicured gardens on a beachfront property. It was such a luxury to stay there. I cherished every moment in that paradise.

During the days I wrote in my journal, swam, lay in the sun and marveled at the new landscape. At nights I turned on the music loudly and danced my ass off, naked and glowing.

But it was the valley that was calling me, not this gorgeous house. So after a few days I packed my backpack and started the hike into the valley. It was a long hike in, about eight hours of crazily treacherous trails, at times with drop-offs that went hundreds of feet straight down onto rocks near the sea. But it was breathtaking and magical and I felt like unicorns were around every bend.

When I arrived in the valley, I met three people right away who became my companions: Cosmo, Star and Luna. They had never met each other before now, but they were my constellation of friends for the next couple of weeks. Cosmo was a man who lived on another island and came to Kauai on a pilgrimage of sorts to visit a sacred site. His spiritual teacher had channeled the core of her teachings from a mountaintop on Kauai and he planned to visit that mountaintop soon. Luna was a fifty-year-old woman from China who embarked several years before on a spiritual quest to find Truth. This led her all over the world, from meeting the Dalai Lama to joining the Christian Church and now to Nature, which she was hoping to connect within this valley. And then there was Star, a twenty-three-year-old girl from New Jersey, whose blue eyes shone with wonder as she danced around in bliss all the time, with her feet barely touching the ground.

That evening a large group of people were gathering for a shared meal. I followed my new companions into the forest on hidden trails and was amazed to find out how many people were living out there in the valley. I met one man who had been there for over twenty-five years living under a tarp. Some, like myself, were only there temporarily; and there was every type of person in between.

As I was walking through the warm jungle towards the gathering, I rounded a corner and almost ran into a man coming towards me. I looked up and immediately recognized him – from *somewhere*.

I had never seen him before. That was clear. He was in his sixties with a head of long white hair and a full white beard. He had a big belly, strong chest, a jungle print sarong wrapped around his waist with wiry muscular legs protruding from the bottom. But although I did not recognize his physical form, I knew him. I knew him well. He looked at me with the same recollection, and we just stood in front of one another looking into each other's eyes with emotion, confusion, recognition and even love. A deep knowing.

We introduced ourselves and began to talk about where we knew each other from. We shared our life experiences, and our conversation was deep from the start. It seemed other-worldly. And within a few moments we were talking about our brushes with death. I told him about the seizure I had from the Cerebral Cysticercosis, and then something dawned on us at the same time.

We remembered.

We knew each other from *that place*. That white light place. That place where we were given a choice. Or a directive.

I remembered stepping into a space made of white light, or energy, rather. There were other beings there. We did not have bodies but we could see each other, or know each other fully without even speaking to each other. Yet voices were not needed in this place.

We were convening, waiting to meet with someone or some thing. As I waited for my meeting, I took in all that was around me: the few other souls, the vast expanse of infinite beautiful energy. Everything seemed so alive, as alive as can be. Not dying life, like plants, but infinite life. Energy that will never die. I was also like that in this place.

My time came to meet with the One. I was told that my work on earth had not finished. I was invited to go back and fulfill my purpose in this life. Although I sensed I had a choice, of course I would choose what was suggested.

So I left. I went back into my body and I saw that place no more.

And Michael was there. We were there at the same time. And our souls knew each other from that place. He had taken a fall down a cliff many years ago and had broken his neck. And was told by the One, while he was lying there dying that he was also not finished. So he chose to return, and to live his purpose. He was miraculously discovered and brought to a hospital where the doctors told him he was lucky to be alive. And lucky to walk again.

We cried when we told each other of this place and these memories. They were truly memories of a time I did not recall until that moment when the visions came flooding back to me clearly. We wept as we hugged and could not believe what we were telling each other. I had a feeling that there were only a few other souls there when I was there, and he was definitely one of them. I wondered if I would ever meet the others? Perhaps on the spiral path, when I need another reminder.

At the potluck, someone had either brought a goat in on a kayak or they had found it there in the valley. I wasn't sure. But a huge barbecue was happening and people brought other dishes to collectively create a feast. Cosmo began telling me more about his spiritual beliefs, which were deeply rooted in quantum physics, but even for me, were really out there. He spoke of crystals and aliens and all sorts of things. Because of my physics background his stories were interesting. I was totally fascinated. He also told me that the woman who channeled the information he believed was also named Ashanna, though she spelled it a bit differently.

I spent the following weeks learning where the hidden gardens were in the valley. I learned what watercress looked like growing wild next to the river so I could pick it each day and have a salad. I made my own fires each night to cook over and generally just sat in absolute awe of the beauty of this paradise. Rainbows appeared several times daily and made the isolated beach seem totally magical. There was a long waterfall that came from a spring at the top of a verdant cliff, so the water was both the most delicious fresh drinking water I had ever tasted, and the most enlivening shower I had ever experienced. The ocean was gentle and glowing turquoise, the sand was white and clean, the air even cleaner and the forest was full of amazing wild growth with fruit and flowers dripping from the trees. The only thing about this slice of paradise that did not seem dreamy were the helicopters. They littered the sky, filled with tourists several times a day who could not or would not make the walk into this beautiful valley but wanted to see it from above. The helicopters seemed like loud polluting mosquitoes that I never seemed to get used to. I was continually put off by these gas-guzzling machines, so out of place in this otherwise totally natural environment.

I continued to learn from my atmospheric companions. Star was so present and floaty; a bit hard for me to connect with at times, but I loved the way she was absolutely aware and in the moment. Luna had amazing stories of her spiritual search and I loved to sit at her feet and learn about this strong committed soul sister who escaped a stiff and limiting conservative culture in a small village in China to roam the world in search of Truth and Beauty. Cosmo looked and acted just like Jesus Christ. He was tall with long brown hair, big blue eyes and walked barefoot everywhere he went as he spread positive energy and support. He was about to leave the valley to go to the mountaintop where his spiritual teacher, my namesake, had her "download." He asked me if I wanted to accompany him on his journey. Of course I wanted to go! Of course I did! How could I not want to go to a mountaintop with Jesus Christ to the spot where another woman named Ashanna downloaded quantum physics laden–spiritual messages about aliens?

We walked out on the same trail we came in on, and then hitchhiked to the home of one of his friends, a man who also followed this woman's teachings. His name was Tristan Two-Whales. He was a massage therapist, healer and a gentle, sweet man. After a good sleep we woke and made the trek to the base of the mountain. When we arrived, we learned from a ranger that floods had caused the land around the mountain to become very boggy and it was not crossable. We looked at each other with confused and disappointed glances. It seemed like an anticlimax to all of us but there was nothing we could do. We looked at the mountaintop from afar and turned around to go our separate ways.

After saying my goodbyes and giving gratitude to Cosmo and Tristan Two-Whales, I visited a health food store and refilled my backpack with dried food. I hitchhiked to the trail head and walked back into the valley for a second time. When I made the hike in I kept seeing two people on the trail in front of me who wore earth-colored wraps around their tanned lean bodies, barefoot with waist-length dreadlocks twisted up on their heads. It was a couple that looked alike and they were rather beautiful. There was a glow around both of them in a way I had never seen before. They seemed like little fairies, unreal creatures from a distant time but looked so right in this magical place. Later on, I met them in the valley; the man was English and the woman was Australian. They had gone to India in their teens to travel, study yoga and meditation, met each other there and never left until recently. They were full-on yogis who lived on a mountainside under the stars, owned nothing but what they wore and had only a copper cooking pot, a knife and some odds-and-ends utensils that were bound up in a tan cloth on their backs. They had surrendered fully to the path of yoga and had left the modern world behind in order to do so. I was fascinated by these two souls who had the courage to live such an ascetic lifestyle.

I sat around their fire nightly asking them questions about their lives, about their beliefs, about all sorts of things. How do you get food on the mountain where you live? What do you meditate on? What do you do, I asked the woman, when you have your period? What do you think about astrology? Do you like to dance? How do you really spend your time? How do you get by without a job? How do you even afford to come to Hawaii? To this question the man answered calmly, "When you live in this way, the money will come." Mmmm. I had a good think on that one.

One day they asked me to join them for a sweat lodge and I readily accepted. We went into the wilderness where an existing lodge had been built and we foraged to collect fallen wood. After we had a sizable pile we made a huge fire, placed some stones in it and then held a sweat lodge that lasted all afternoon. We would emerge periodically to jump in the river, then return to the heat. It was, as sweat lodges tend to be, cleansing, intense and impossible to be anywhere else in the mind other than the present moment.

While I was in the valley I felt Spirit running thick in me. When I went to sleep at night I felt something flow through my body that I called "Spirit." I am not sure what it was, exactly. I would wake up in the middle of the night and find my body turned to the side and I would not feel the flow. Then when I pointed my feet towards the ocean, the flow would begin again and I would go back to sleep peacefully. Experiencing Spirit so clearly there, I felt my prayers were heard and answered. When I prayed for clarity for the next step in my life, I got a clear answer that I was supposed to go back to California and start a holistic health school. I envisioned running a detox program that offered guidance as well as community support for people going through a cleanse. When I did the big detox with the naturopathic doctor years before, it was amazing but I felt alone, and it was hard to keep myself accountable to the strict diet. I craved community and some sort of forum to share my experiences and ask questions. I also envisioned a class to support those who wanted to make sustainable healthy lifestyle changes after their cleanse was finished. I felt Spirit tell me to go back and create something for people with similar needs. It felt like I was charged with this duty to manifest these ideas and I needed to return to California to do it.

One morning the yogis hiked up to my tent and told me they were leaving. Instead of saying "good-bye," one of them said, "I'll see you on the path," as they waved and walked away. I smiled and understood.

I never kept in touch with them, but years later I took my first trip to India. Within my first twenty-four hours of being in that enchanting and complex country with billions of people, I saw the two yogis from Kauai. Yes, I did see them on the path. Amazing.

I felt like my time in the beautiful valley was coming to an end as well, so after breakfast that morning I started to pack up my belongings. On the walk out I wanted to sing. I thought about prayers to sing, some sort of spiritual song that matched what I was feeling, what I believed. I started to sing *Amazing Grace* but when I got to that part where I called myself a "wretch," I stopped. I realized it no longer matched what I believed. I did not, with all my heart, believe that I was a wretch any more. I did not believe that I was unworthy of God's love — what does that even mean, anyway? Is that even possible? At that point it started raining. It was a light rain; a rain that enveloped me in the warm air and a song started pouring through me. This was the first song I ever wrote:

Joy, and blessings, abundance and love
Oh come and rain, rain, rain, rain
Down on my soul.
Joy, and blessings, abundance and love
Oh come and rain, rain, rain, rain
Down on my soul.
Come and rain, rain, rain, rain.
Come and rain, rain, rain, rain.
Come and rain, rain, rain, rain.
Come and rain, rain, rain, rain.
Rain on my body, rain on my mind.
Rain on my spirit, unified.
Rain on my body, rain on my mind,
Oh come and rain, rain, rain, rain, unified.

When I reached the road I put up my thumb to hitch a ride to the airport. I had a day and a half to make the journey and it was only a few hours drive, but I needed to make sure I would make it. Suddenly a car drove up next to me and when I looked inside I saw that it was Star. She had left the valley a few weeks before, around the time I hiked out with Cosmo, and had been given a car by her mother. She was house-sitting for a friend and took me there to spend the night. It was a huge, gorgeous, luxurious home. Some of her other friends were there too, making music: playing the guitar, the didgeridoo, a flute and a couple of drums. We had an amazing jam session, then made a beautiful dinner and sat in the hot tub under the stars and relaxed.

Who ever said you needed a bag of money to have a magnificent holiday in Hawaii?

I left the beautiful house the next morning and said my goodbyes to Star and her friends. I again went to the road to begin hitchhiking towards the airport.

The man that picked me up asked me if I had some time before my flight left. I actually had tons of time. He told me he would take me all the way to the airport but he had a detour he wanted to make and asked me if I would like to accompany him. I had a good feeling about him right away so I said yes. He was a small man in his late fifties, and he had a genuinely peaceful feeling to him. We drove off the road into the wilderness for a while, and he explained to me that he was part of an organization that was trying to help keep the wisdom of the Kahunas alive. Apparently the Kahunas, the ancient medicine people of Hawaii, had historically passed on their wisdom to others by taking on young disciples, but as their culture was becoming westernized the teachings were dying out. He explained that we were driving onto sacred land to meet with one of these Kahunas.

When we parked I got out of the car and started walking towards the big man sitting in the forest. He rose, looked directly into my eyes and held out his hand. He said to me, "This is for you. I have dreamt about you coming to me for three days now and I made this for you from the land." It was a necklace made from some of the stone that was strewn about, showing a hint of the architecture that used to stand on this land. The stones had small crystals inside that shone in the sunlight and were hanging from a rope he had made from the bark of one of the trees by stripping the bark into fibers, then rolling it on his lower leg to form a small string. There was a shell on top of the stone as well, and some wood from a nearby tree at the end of the string keeping the knot secure. It was simple but beautiful, and I was amazed by his words and his gift.

He told me to follow him, which I did. He led me through the woods and took me to a large pyramidal rock that was much taller than me and quite large at the base. He asked me to stand at a particular spot in front of the rock and told me about a sacred triangle on the island. He told me that I was standing at one of the points, and then he pointed into the distance at a large mountain, shaped exactly like the rock I was standing in front of. He told me that that mountain (which happened to be the exact same mountain that Cosmo and I had tried to hike, where my namesake had channeled the information), the land where I was standing in front of this rock, and the valley I had just come from, formed a sacred triune on the island – all connected.

Now this man didn't know anything about me. I hadn't said a word about having been in the valley, or of Cosmo and the attempted journey to that mountain. But there I was, in front of this towering rock, completing a mysterious pilgrimage of my own to the sacred triune of the island. I stood there in awe, feeling Spirit so thickly that it made the hairs on the back of my neck stand on end.

We walked back to the man who drove me there, and he and the Kahuna talked about the program while I walked around the forest feeling the energy of the beautiful land and reflecting on what the Kahuna had just said to me. They eventually wrapped up their meeting and asked me if I would like to join them in going to a local healing center. As I had a secured ride to the airport in time for my flight, I was delighted to accept their invitation. I had heard of the healing center they spoke of but had never been to it. When we arrived, the woman who owned the place smiled, as she was good friends with both of the men. She led us to our own room complete with massage tables, a fountain and beautiful flowers. I took a look at the massage table and asked the Kahuna if he would like a healing session from me. He accepted gratefully, and we spent the next several hours giving and receiving healing, as well as sharing about our lives and spiritual philosophies. He looked up at me at one point and said to me in a clear, strong voice, "Hawaii is your home. Go back to

California and do whatever you need to do, but when you finish, come back home."

I loved every moment I spent in that sacred healing center. And I accepted the Kahuna's advice, love and gifts with gratitude. I left him after giving him a big, familial hug and went to the airport. To this day that necklace sits on my altar, and I still wonder if I will return to Hawaii as he suggested.

Chapter 10

Darkness

When I returned to California I found a great home to move into through a friend, and began putting together the holistic health courses I had envisioned. I gathered together an amazing staff of teachers and therapists and we spent a couple of months meeting, getting to know each other and putting together the first course we were going to lead. We filled the course with students, rented a place to hold the classes and began teaching. It went well and our staff members were absolutely incredible.

But as the weeks went by I started to slip into a depression again. The slope was again a slippery one and the days just got darker. It got to the point that I was having a difficult time even getting to the classes and I felt the darkness come over me. I felt like a helpless victim to these dark spells and I did not know what to do.

The months passed and darkness grew. Day after day went by, sending me a little further under the covers. My life started to fall apart as I was no longer able to participate in anything any more. I dissolved the business I had spent months building just as it was all set up to run with very little work. I had no drive anymore and I began to feel totally uncomfortable around people in general. I sequestered myself in my room, and eventually under my covers. This feeling was familiar to me, as it was similar to the depression I felt when I first moved to San Francisco some years before.

My roommate Thea was an angel. She came into my room every now and then, and just laid down next to me, put her arm around me and talked to me softly. She checked on me often and brought me food if I needed it, or visitors if I could handle it. She was the truest of friends and I will never forget the kindness she bestowed on me during that dark time.

I still made it to acupuncture and the naturopathic doctor's appointments and took the herbs with desperation, yet nothing was helping. Eventually I started to see how much this condition was affecting not only my life but also the people around me – my family, my friends, my roommates, Thea. I couldn't even support myself financially any more. Something had to give.

At that point I decided it was time to start taking the medication recommended to me by the psychiatrist from Stanford. I went to see him and he put me on an antidepressant. I don't know why, but I felt like a failure for taking the drug. I had so much strange emotion wrapped up around taking a pill for depression. I felt like I wasn't good enough or complete on my own, and had to rely on a drug company to make me feel normal. I don't know why I didn't feel that way about the acupuncture or the herbs, but for some reason it felt different. But I was at the end of my rope and I was desperate for some help, so I took it.

Weeks after I started taking the antidepressant, the darkness was still upon me. I got on a plane to see my parents in Georgia for a routine family visit. It was during this trip, actually, that the drug kicked in. All of a sudden I started to feel myself return and in just a few days my whole family said that it seemed like I was back. I had strength and energy coursing through me again, and it literally felt like a floor came up to meet my feet so I could walk again. I felt an energetic ground beneath me that wasn't there before, as if I could no longer dip so low anymore. I got excited. I could start living a normal life again!

The first thing that entered my mind was that I wanted to go back to school after having put it off for so long. So before I even left Georgia, I contacted the naturopathic medical school I had wanted to attend for so long and arranged to begin that summer. Just the thought of starting that next chapter in my life infused me with even more excitement and joy every day, and I seemed like a totally different person when I returned to California. I had just enough time there to gather my belongings, buy a car and move my buns up to Seattle. Thea went with me and helped me find a small apartment near the gorgeous campus before she left for home. And thus the next chapter of my life began.

I studied the sciences, Tai Chi and Ayurvedic medicine that semester. I lived in a crappy apartment, really, but it was right on a stream that fed into Lake Washington and there was a dock right outside my door. I routinely took out a small boat that belonged to a neighbor and rowed myself up and down the little river. When I wasn't on the river or in class, I rode my bike down a long bike path that was also right outside my door and weaved its way through fields while hot air balloons often decorated the sky.

I enjoyed this life close to nature, combined with the focus of the studies. I fell in love with Ayurvedic medicine and began going to an Ayurvedic doctor from India who ran a school in Seattle. I started to receive treatments from him and followed a strict Ayurvedic diet. This medicine system felt so right to me that I started doubling up, taking classes in Ayurveda with his institute as well as classes at the naturopathic medical school. I got back into meditation and yoga. I was feeling absolutely wonderful.

By the second semester I was convinced that I could wean myself off the antidepressant drugs as long as I kept the rest of my life like it was – stable. I still had so much emotional charge wrapped up in the fact that I was taking the pills. I was ashamed and never wanted anyone to find out, especially in that type of school. I also thought it was just kind of bad for me in some way too, and if I could keep the Ayurvedic treatments and healthy lifestyle choices up, I thought I could take myself off of it. Just like the anti-seizure medicine, I made a pact with myself that I would watch myself closely, and if I needed it again I would start taking it. But if I didn't actually need it and I could live without it, then I would.

I started to take less and less of the dosage each day. After a while, I stopped taking it all together and thought I would go cold turkey for the rest of the dosage I was still taking.

It was terrible.

For days I was rocking back and forth feeling as though a loud CD was skipping in my head. I had sensations in my face that felt like there were a million microscopic strings attached to the inside of my skin yanking backwards every few seconds. I literally felt the skin on my face implode backwards, coinciding with the sounds of the CD skipping in my head. I would stand in front of the mirror and stare at myself, sure that I would see my skin being pulled backwards again and again – but there was nothing to see.

It was a trick of the mind and yet it felt so real.

I basically holed up in my home going through this horrendous experience alone – enduring it. I could do nothing: not read, not talk to anyone and not even think, it seemed. It just kept going. Hour after hour. It was horrible.

Days slipped by, and then finally I woke one morning to find that it was finished.

A couple of weeks later I began to have severe pain in the same place that had hurt so bad in Thailand, the spot where I had received emergency surgery in Bangkok and then later a bigger surgery in Colorado.

I went to a doctor in Seattle who asked to see my medical records from the surgery I had had in Denver. I was in his office while he was looking through them and he said, "Well, I see here that the doctor decided to put a rubber drain into your body during the surgery. But I don't see any record of it being taken out. When did you get that drain removed?"

"Drain?" I asked. "What drain?"

It turned out that during the surgery four years ago, the doctor decided to put a drain into the site of my surgery to continue the drainage of fluids from the tumor to the outside of my body via my intestine. It was supposed to have been removed days or at most, a few weeks afterwards, but I was never told that it was put in. I was asleep during the surgery and I remember waking up, getting sick from the anesthesia and vomiting, putting on my clothes and leaving the hospital.

I was never told to come back or that I needed to do anything.

So I just went on living my life.

My new doctor in Seattle explained that my body had either enveloped the drain and broken it down inside my body, or rejected it over time and pushed it out. Either way the wound site never healed properly and as a result I had a tennis ball-sized tumor sitting outside my large intestine and he needed to do surgery right away.

Within a few days I was under anesthesia again and under the knife. When I awoke they told me that they were only able to drain it a little, and I was going to need six more surgeries over the next six months to continue draining it, before finally removing the shell of the tumor after the last surgery.

I was devastated.

I was totally out of it after that first surgery.

I was sore, sick and bed-ridden.

I had to put pads down on the bed to catch all the blood, keep a bucket next to the bed to catch my vomit and it hurt like hell to go to the bathroom.

I could barely walk.

I knew the next six months were going to revolve around hospital visits for six more surgeries.

I withdrew from my classes at the naturopathic medical school and the Ayurvedic Institute and moved back to Colorado to be close to my brother. I felt that I needed to be near someone who could take care of me during these surgeries. I packed up as best as I could, despite the fact that I was still sore and bleeding, and drove across the country over ice and snow to arrive in Boulder, Colorado.

I went to another surgeon to get a second opinion and he told me an even scarier story than the first. He said that instead of six more surgeries he wanted to perform one huge one, but to get to the site of the tumor he would need to cut through my anal sphincter muscle, possibly resulting in my being incontinent for the rest of my life, thus having to wear a diaper and not being in control of my bowels.

With such a bleak future to look forward to, in the dead of winter, leaving my studies and new friends in Seattle, I started to get depressed again.

I went to a naturopathic doctor right away. I loved him right from the start. He had high hopes for me to reduce the number of surgeries needed or maybe avoid them altogether using natural healing modalities. But in order for me to do that, I needed the strength to take care of myself by completing a cleanse and exercising, amongst other things.

At that point I was so depressed I could not take care of myself at all. He explained that although he normally didn't encourage people to take allopathic medications he suggested that I start taking the antidepressant again. So I did.

I went back to the hospital in Denver where I had that first surgery to get any documents I could about what had happened, and why I wasn't told about the drain being put in my body. They looked in my file and gave me the documentation that they had. It showed that the nurses were supposed to call me after the surgery, explain the fact that the drain was put inside of me, and make my next appointment to have it checked or removed.

The record showed that they called once and there was "no answer".

And that was that.

There was no message left, no second call attempted.

Somebody had dropped the ball.

I found a malpractice lawyer and met with him. He took a look at the documents I had and listened to my story. He said to me, "Unfortunately,

I have bad news for you. If you lived in another state, you would have a good case on your hands. However, Colorado has the strictest laws on malpractice in the country. If I took this case on I would spend more money on court fees than the amount of money you would get out of it. If you had a colostomy bag you had to wear for the rest of your life, then maybe we could get something, but six surgeries? It's not worth my time."

Wow.

What do you do with that?

Just as before, about three weeks after I started taking the antidepressant, I started to spin up and out of the dark depression and had enough energy to do the things I needed to do. In this case it was cleansing, exercising, taking herbs, going to my healing appointments, going to the sauna, meditating and going deep inside myself to find the things that needed healing. I believed that the tumor in my gut wasn't just a physical thing, but had emotional components as well. I was determined to holistically heal my body.

I found a therapist in town who had been a medical doctor for many years before becoming a therapist. She specialized in working with people who had strange medical conditions and/or conditions that didn't seem to heal. Considering that I was dealing with the emotional aftermath of the Cerebral Cysticercosis, which most therapists had never heard of nor understood, plus the tumor outside my colon, I chose her.

We connected right away. She was good at what she did and believed in what she was doing.

In our therapy sessions we talked about things that had a lot of emotional charge for me – my seizure episodes, my experiences in the hospitals, the surgeries. When my speech would get faster and I would start to show emotion about something, we would stop the conversation and switch to thinking about something that brought me peace.

At the time I had a Columbian red-tailed boa constrictor as a pet, which was one of the most calm and exotic animals I had ever seen. She was gorgeous. So I chose to think of her each time we stopped for one of these breaks. After a few minutes of "sourcing," we resumed the story right where I left off, and although I was talking about the same thing it had lost some of the charge. The objective, she explained, was to undo the circuitry in the brain that twisted these experiences together with fear and emotional charge, and break up that negative spiral with positive, peaceful memories.

I could feel it working.

I also found a Reiki group that met in town and received some powerful healing sessions from them. I had been certified as a Reiki Master many years prior and thought that this energy therapy would help. Reiki is an ancient Japanese healing technique in which the practitioner opens up as a vessel for universal energy to flow through their hands into the recipient, thus activating the natural healing process of the body. During these organized Reiki circles, people would take turns lying on the table receiving healing, and then we would switch.

I always felt better after these sessions.

My appointments with the naturopathic doctor were amazing as well. He was also an acupuncturist and gave me sessions two or three times a week. He led me through a cleanse that became progressively deeper over time. He gave me a protein-rich powder that I mixed with water or juice that helped my body reduce inflammation. Besides these detox smoothies, I only ate fruit, vegetables, tea, veggie broth and lots of water. I was diligent about exercise as well. I had a lot resting on the fact that I did.

I did not want to face going into another surgery, not to mention six.

The next time I went in to see the surgeon he was amazed. He said that it was a "miracle" and not only did I not need any more surgeries but I had healed so quickly from the first one he could hardly tell that I had even had it.

He washed up, left the room and just like that it was over.

I looked over to the nurse who was still standing in the room and she had a look of astonishment on her face. Her eyes were open wide and she said, "He has never said anything like that to anyone before. That is incredible!"

I drove home in tears of gratitude and immediately called the naturopath and therapist to share the good news. We all celebrated.

The healing sessions continued, though. Just because I no longer needed a surgery didn't mean that the cause of it all was gone, and I wanted to be sure that it would be all rooted out. So the work continued.

Chapter 11

> ⤙⤚

Breakdown

Over the next few weeks, I began to lose sleep. At first it was a little at a time, making me tired throughout the day. I would lie in bed and my mind would race, thinking about colors, spatial math problems, symbols and architecture. Then my mind started to spin during the days too, faster and faster. I began to think about the physics I studied in college and I wanted to learn more. I actually hungered for it with a rabid appetite. I went to the library all the time and checked out books on fractals, quantum physics, codes and sacred geometry. I had had an interest in these things for a long time, but now I was up all hours of the night reading about them, but never the same topic for very long. My attention span was short but my mind was ravenous. I think I had twenty books checked out from the library all at once.

Besides all the books lying in piles all over my apartment, I also started collecting river stones. During my sleepless nights, I built little stone towers called cairns all over the house. For hours on end I would get into a zone and build, tear down and rebuild, delicately balancing my little stone towers. I built the cairns in geometric patterns and constantly moved them around to make new fractal shapes or 3D art. Sometimes I would move my belongings around my little apartment according to the color they were, and I was in a continual state of trying to balance everything by height, color, texture and energy. I had to make sure that there wasn't too much of one color in one area, and that the placement of each piece of furniture, each plant leaf, each article of clothing laying about was placed in such a way that it balanced everything, and my eye was always looking out for the thing that was bringing things out of balance. It became an obsession.

I also began to pour over my own medical records and MRIs. I had moved so many times, and had seen so many doctors over the years, that somewhere along the way I had been given a copy of my medical records and films to share with the new doctors I went to see. What I read freaked me out.

The reports said, "Multiple enhanced lesions in the brain." "Ring-enhancing lesions approximately 4 cm in diameter involving the superficial brain adjacent to the anterior right sylvian fissure, in two locations in the left temporal lobe." And so it went on and on. Imagine reading those words over and over and over…

One doctor described Cerebral Cysticercosis "as if you have suffered an internal gunshot wound to the brain," and described how a bullet spreads out upon impact, and how similar it is to the path the worms had taken in my brain and the spaces they had squished and killed in order to grow. Those words would repeat in my mind as I looked over my MRI films at the worms scattered throughout my brain. They were everywhere. They were easy to see. The ones with swelling around them were circled by the doctors in a special pencil.

I also thought about what the infectious disease doctors had explained to me, that the worms were throughout my entire brain and it was unknown how they might affect me in future.

"This could change your personality or change your intelligence," they said, so since then I was constantly watching myself. Was my personality changing? It seemed like it was always changing to some degree. How much of that was just life and how much of that was due to the worms? Those thoughts were so outlandish and terrible and I would work myself into a frenzy of fear and anxiety, never being able to answer those questions.

I didn't know what to do. I needed sleep but could not drift off no matter how long I laid in bed. It started to get out of control. But at the time, I didn't know what was going on with me. I was so absorbed in my own experience it did not occur to me to call a doctor.

Once, I missed a couple of nights of sleep in a row and called my little brother. I was freaking out, speaking nonsense. He could tell I was in a state of panic and that something was wrong. Although it was late, he began worrying about me and drove over to my apartment while we were on the phone. After spending a while in his calming presence, I began to get tired and finally fell asleep. He left and drove home in the middle of the night.

After that good sleep, I then spent night after night (How many? I cannot tell.) without sleeping a wink, building rock cairns all over my house, reading my books about codes and number theory, arranging and rearranging my belongings.

One cold morning after the sun rose, I felt that I needed to calm down. I was worried about myself and could not make my body and mind slow down. I left my house and walked to the meditation center nearby. I had meditated with them many times during prior months and thought that the calm would help me.

I could tell that my mind was spinning out of control.

Their doors were locked. It was just after dawn and the town was mostly still asleep.

I saw a policeman's car parked nearby and I began to walk over to ask for help, not knowing what I needed exactly but that I just didn't feel good. As I walked up behind his car he drove away, not knowing I was coming to him. So I turned and started walking down to the local yoga studio. I was not dressed for yoga and had no money on me, but I was desperate for something to calm me down and didn't know what else to do.

I ended up getting distracted on the way and went into the outdoor patio area of a local coffee shop.

This is when I really started to lose my mind.

I sat down next to a man and started to discuss life in the strangest ways. I looked around me and started to feel like everyone was in a play and that all these people knew each other.

I felt like I was the only one not clued into the performance they were all giving. Giving for whom? Me? I wasn't sure. But I would see someone dialing a cell phone and then hear a phone ring behind me a second later. I was convinced that all these people were calling each other and that everything was somehow choreographed and rehearsed, except for me sitting in the middle.

I started to speak nonsense disturbing the people around me.

I made my way to a couple with a little boy sitting at a nearby table. I was sure that they had rented the little boy for tax purposes and it occurred to me what a great idea that was. I went up to them and asked them where they had rented him, as if I was going to go to the little kid shop and rent one for myself for the tax break.

My brain actually came up with this stuff and I believed it was real.

Then somehow my brain took a turn and I started asking the woman if her partner was secretly looking at porn (he was sitting right there). I asked her if she thought it was possible if someone had taken photographs of me nude without me knowing and had posted them on the internet, and if her partner was looking at them at night without her knowing? This seemingly innocent and honest question brought her to tears and they got up from the table and went inside the cafe.

I followed them in and got distracted again by the line to get coffee. I decided I wanted to get a cup of coffee, too. While I was in line I saw the man from the couple outside go talk to the owner of the shop and tell her what had just happened. She came up to me directly and asked me politely to leave the premises.

I didn't quite understand why I was asked to leave, but I went outside anyway.

At that point I saw a toy that belonged to the little boy that I thought the couple had "rented." I didn't want him to lose his toy, so I snuck back inside to give it to them.

I never got the toy to the couple.

The shop owner saw me, called the police and then forced me to go outside.

Within a minute or two there was a police officer there to arrest me for trespassing or disturbing the peace or something. He asked me to follow him and get into his car but I did not understand what was happening to me and I tried to run away. He ran after me, forced me into handcuffs and put me into the backseat of his car. I started to tell him that my family had loads of money and asked if he would let me go if they paid him enough. Then I became totally convinced that all my friends (I didn't have too many in Boulder at that point) had organized a party at the police station where the officer was taking me, and when I arrived, everyone was going to pop out and yell, "Surprise!" I became convinced it was all a set-up and I was going to a party! I was so excited. When I arrived at the police station I started asking the policemen where they had gotten their costumes because I truly didn't think they were real police officers.

I was checked in and taken to a small room.

I was talking such nonsense that they strapped my arms and legs to a chair and left me alone for a long time.

I sat. I sang – and I started to hallucinate.

I sang the Namibian national anthem loudly as if I was a soldier.

I looked around trying to figure out where my friends that were throwing the party were.

A little while later, I yelled out for help.

All of a sudden I thought I was pregnant and was going into labor. But nobody came to help me.

So I had to give birth alone.

I had the experience of birthing three children in a row, right there onto the floor. I could feel them come out and land on the floor, but they were not really babies, just puddles on the floor.

My "babies" were puddles of some type of liquid (there was actually nothing on the floor) and I became distressed because I was strapped to the chair and couldn't pick up my newborns. I don't know how much time passed and in what order things happened, but here is what I remember:

People came into the room, one after another, to ask me my name, address and birth date.

At this point I was totally dissociated, and I had no idea who I really was.

I thought to myself, "What is my name?" I truly thought my name was Jesus. So that is what I answered.

Then they asked me when I was born.

Instead of trying to think of a birth date like usual, I tried to remember being born and then tried to figure out when that was. However, I could remember living for so long – so, so long. I could remember generations of people coming and going, past the point when people were even here on the earth. I could remember when the earth was formed, and as I sat remembering the entire history of the universe, I realized that I was never born. It was infinity behind me. Never a beginning. So that is what I told them.

"I was never born. I have been here forever."

The next person to ask me my name got a different answer.

This time I thought I was Hitler. So that is what I said. And I believed it with all my heart. To me, Jesus was ultimate love, and Hitler was ultimate fear and horror. And I had it all inside me, without judgment.

The whole human spectrum and infinity – in me – as me.

Later, yet another person came in to ask me my name. I looked down at the badge of the person asking me and it said "E." So then I thought we were playing a game and I thought her name was "E." I started to say letters as if they were my name, too. Well, if her name was "E" then my name could have been "O" or "B."

It was at this point that I started to realize that I was really locked up.

I had the thought that the government had taught all these people a code language. I thought you had to say things in a particular order while simultaneously saying something else with your nervous system and body language.

I thought that if I could figure out how to use this code, and answer in the right way then they would let me go.

If someone introduced himself as Wilbur, my thought process went something like this: "Wilbur, Wilbur – Wilbur was in *Charlotte's Web*, which I had read in first grade and in first grade I sat next to Jason who was friends with Ted. Ted's sister was Jamie and she had red hair so they must want me to say red." So if they asked me when I was born, I would somehow make my body feel like I was saying *Charlotte's Web* while my lips uttered the word "red."

So for every single question they posed, my brain would link a stream of conscious thoughts in a crazy string.

And then I would try in vain to say one thing with my nervous system (whatever that means, but that is what I was doing).

And another with my body language.

And another thing from my mouth.

All at the same time.

After a while they brought in a phlebotomist to take my blood to see what kind of drug I was on. When the results came back that I was not on anything (such as meth or LSD) they put me in an ambulance.

And sent me to a mental hospital.

I was put in a solitary room.

This room had nothing but a pad on a metal slab for a bed.

There was no toilet, which forced me to go to the bathroom all over the floor.

I had not eaten much the days before, and what I had eaten was not balanced or nutritious so my stomach was a bit off. I was so distressed about using the bathroom on the floor, but when I couldn't hold it any longer I just had to squat and pee and have diarrhea – all over the floor.

A few minutes later a nurse came in to clean it all up, which sent me into feeling an immense amount of guilt and shame.

But I couldn't help it. I continued to feel sick.

And although I tried to hold it in as long as I could, eventually I had to go again – and again – all over the floor. And each time a nurse came in to wipe up my mess.

It was torturous.

Then I realized I was extremely thirsty. I became desperate for water. But for whatever reason, they would not give me more than a single little cup.

I didn't understand where I was and I became fearful that I was going to actually die from thirst.

The walls were padded.

The door was locked.

I completely panicked.

They kept me locked up for a long time – and I went through waves of stress and fatigue – but I still couldn't sleep.

I wandered around the room and pounded on the door.

A few times a nurse came in and explained to me that they wanted to take me away to another place.

She told me not to panic.

Two large men came on either side of me and grabbed my arms.

At first I started to walk with them, but then I freaked out, completely fearful of where they were taking me, and who they were. They were very large men and I became overwhelmed with terror that they were going to torture me or take me someplace underground. When I struggled against them they left me alone rather than force me – and they left me in the padded room. For a long, long time.

And finally, finally, after so long…

I fell asleep on the padded metal slab.

When I woke, the two strong men came back and grabbed my arms again. They were taking me out of the room, but at that point I was relaxed and limp. I surrendered to wherever they were going to take me. I felt I could not get out.

I was taken to a room full of doctors. Although I felt foggy and really out of it, my mind had calmed down after the much needed sleep. I was able to give them my real name and medical history. They typed some things into a computer and checked the system to verify this information and read my medical records. They continued to ask me questions for a while, and then they immediately gave me some Tegretol, the one drug that was found to control the hallucinatory, complex partial seizures I had had years before.

Within a few hours of taking that little pill, I was back on earth, totally lucid.

Despite the terrible and confusing past days I was back to normal. Yet, understandably so, they kept me in the hospital for several more days, which was extremely disturbing and stressful.

Everyone that was there was totally mad in varying degrees, like I had been. Someone that I thought was nice and pretty normal, after talking to me about what a lovely day it was outside, all of a sudden broke out into a screaming fit about nonsense. And my roommate started screaming that night. When the nurses came in, she was yelling that I was using the bathroom too much and had stolen her toothbrush, which wasn't true at all.

I had just come down off of a totally psychotic episode, trying with all my might to hold onto my sanity, but I was surrounded by insane people screaming and talking nonsense constantly. This would challenge any sane person, but in the fragile state I was in, it was especially hard to be in that hospital.

It was very much like prison.

We were in orange outfits. Our regular clothes were taken away when we were admitted. We were on a tight schedule, forming lines to take our medication three times daily, where we all swallowed different colored pills.

The color pill you took was often a topic of conversation amongst the patients. Like children comparing presents left under the Christmas tree.

We were only allowed outside once or twice a day for twenty minutes at a time in a small courtyard. This happened to be the only time when people could smoke, and almost all of them smoked. I have never been a smoker, and actually have a terrible reaction to second-hand smoke. It makes me nauseous and gives me an immediate headache. So my only allowed times in the precious sunshine with "fresh" air was coupled with clouds of smoke that made me feel very ill. It was terrible.

At some point they decided I was well enough to have visitors, and my brother Travis and his wife came to see me.

When I saw them I felt ridiculous.

I felt like I was in a movie and that what had happened was so surreal it was hard to believe. But they were able to joke with me about it all, and give me love and support in a grounded, solid way.

My time in the mental institution was fascinating. When I got over the acute trauma of the experience and started to really understand that I was going to be released in a few days, I just had to show the staff that I was sane enough to be released, I started to relax and tried to get to know the people around me.

They had amazing stories and were actually sweet, genuinely great people. I started to understand on a fundamental level what a fine line there is between sanity and insanity.

Such a hairline knife-edge.

So easy to fall off on the other side.

I had, at some points in my life, wondered what it was really like inside mental institutions. I had a distant fascination and it intrigued me.

Now I was inside of one. I found out.

I started to take the insane outbursts from the other patients with a grain of salt and became friends with both the patients and the staff. One of the nurses had been a Peace Corps Volunteer in India long ago and we swapped Peace Corps stories. Many of the patients listened to our tales and were intrigued when we showed them on a globe where we had lived.

When they finally released me, I felt like I was actually leaving friends. I thanked the nurses that had cleaned up my excrement when I first arrived.

I thanked the patients that I had gotten to know and truly learned to appreciate.

I thanked all the doctors and nurses that served in that hospital taking care of people that most folks can't stand to be around.

Those nurses are angels, I tell you.

I spent the next couple of weeks at my brother's house. The hospital released me only under the agreement that I would stay with him and be under supervision. After a few long weeks of being away from home, I finally moved back into my apartment. I started seeing my therapist twice a week, had weekly appointments with my psychiatrist and twice-weekly appointments with my acupuncturist. I still had my neurologist, a psycho-pharmacologist, the infectious disease doctors, and Reiki healers. I sat in perpetual self-observation and contemplation. I exercised, cleansed, drank herbal tea and meditated. I spent the whole summer trying to integrate my experience leading up to and including my time in the mental hospital.

My memory of what I had said during that whole psychotic break was quite clear and yet it was so insane that I could hardly believe that it had been me.

It was a surreal time, unsettling to say the least. I had a lot of shame wrapped up around that whole experience of being arrested and taken to a mental institution.

It is a social nightmare – a red flag for anyone seeking a friend. I was afraid to tell anyone. I sequestered myself again, into my own little world with no one but my healers and immediate family allowed inside.

I started seeing a new psychiatrist. He was the opposite of the doctor at Stanford. The Stanford guy was always dressed in a crisp white shirt and tie. The building was silver and shiny and I had to use a big elevator to get to his floor. Everything was large and corporate. His appointments were fifteen minutes long. And you had to say all you could in those brief fifteen minutes because there was another emotionally unstable person right behind you, ready to dump as much as they could in their fifteen-minute slot.

The new doctor in Boulder felt like a warm grandfather. His office was in an old, wooden building and he had red decorative rugs and art from all over the world surrounding a big comfy chair you sat in as you spoke with him. He wore sweater vests and Birkenstocks, and our appointments were an hour long. He delved into my story with interest. (Doctors were always intrigued to talk to someone who had survived Cerebral Cysticercosis. For them, it was something you read about in a textbook but never came across in real life – until I came along.) After he listened to the description of my depression and anxiety over the years, he asked other questions. He asked if I ever felt Spirit unusually strongly, and if I had ever spent tons of money at a time, or conversely, if I had given all my belongings away or something like that. I told him I had never spent a ton of money, that I had never had much of it, and that type of behavior was not something I felt drawn to.

But I told him about the time leading up to and including Hawaii. Yes, I had a very strong connection with Spirit and felt like I was transmitting information from God. I told him how some of my friends came over to get my channeled messages, about how I had gotten a message for myself that I had everything I needed and should give away all my possessions. I relayed the story of how I gave away my car, my clothes, everything, and went to live in the jungles of Hawaii. I told him about the magic that I experienced there.

And after listening to my story with such interest he told me that he thought I had been misdiagnosed all along. It was his opinion that in those brief fifteen-minute sessions with the other doctor, that the psychiatrist at Stanford had not understood what I had experienced fully, and that instead of being depressed, I had bipolar disorder.

In the past, I had been given a prescription for the antidepressant, and he explained to me that that particular medication tends to bring people up out of their darkness, but since I was bipolar, my system had started its climb up into a manic phase, and combined with the antidepressant, it spun out of control into a complete manic episode that sent me into the mental hospital. As it turns out, the Tegretol, which is an anti-seizure medication that ended up stopping all the complex partial seizures I had experienced, was also used to treat bipolar disorder. He reminded me what the infectious disease doctor had told me before, that up to 85% of people with seizures of that magnitude have an emotional disorder afterwards, and that somehow the brain worms and the seizures had affected my brain in this way.

When I left the mental hospital, I continued taking the Tegretol, and this new doctor gave me all sorts of other medications to try as well. I was given some meds to put me to sleep, since the lack of sleep was a large part of the manic episode. But they made me so lethargic in the morning that it was hard to get my day going. His answer to that was to give me a different pill to take in the morning to wake me up. He put me on different types of bipolar medication to take on top of the Tegretol, but as I tried pill after pill, I noticed the side effects more than any help. I ended up leaving all the other pills with him, and just kept taking the Tegretol, practicing my continual self-observation in case any symptoms came up. At least now I knew what to look for as far as depression, anxiety or manic episodes were concerned. I wished that the doctors had told me to look for those symptoms a long time ago, and not just seizures. It's likely that during my time in Hawaii, I was already well into a psychotic episode. So that puts a whole new perspective on my interpretation of my experiences while there. It would also have saved me years of needless suffering, not to mention a stay in the mental hospital.

Chapter 12

Just a Story

It seemed like every day I went to one or two appointments, either therapy or acupuncture or the psychiatrist. I started calling myself a "professional patient." Most people went to school or work but I went to doctors. My daily life was all focused around healing this ever complex and strange illness. After many months of visiting doctors almost every day I began to get antsy. I desperately wanted a change.

I kept getting an intuitive hit to get in touch with the Native American teacher in San Francisco that I did the sweat lodge and vision quest with. He took groups down to Peru every few years, and I kept feeling something inside me telling me to contact him and ask if he was going to Peru any time soon. I couldn't get it out of my mind. I thought about it every day. Finally, one day I called him up and just asked him, and lo and behold, he said he was taking a group soon and I was welcome to go.

I got so excited at the thought of leaving the States for a while, but also immediately felt awash with guilt and fear. I thought that I was "supposed to be healing" and for some reason thought that healing wouldn't happen while I was traveling. I was fearful that the travel would upset the delicate balance I had created for myself. But I felt so strongly that I needed to go, so I decided to trust my intuition. And I joined the group leaving for Peru.

I had no idea how wonderful it would be to leave my daily appointments with different doctors and therapists. I hadn't thought of it before but I spent part of every day telling someone what was wrong with me. I would feel into my thoughts, emotions and body, all parts of me, and describe to them what felt sick. It was as if I was cementing into my daily life the fact that I was ill. When I left Colorado I felt the shift immediately. Despite the good intentions of all my healers and myself, it turned out to be good medicine for me to stop talking about my symptoms all the time and just live my life doing something I enjoyed.

I was living in Boulder and the rest of the people leaving for this journey were in San Francisco. They were gathering regularly before the trip to prepare both emotionally and spiritually. They were praying, setting intentions and beginning to form a tight community. Upon request from the Native American pipe carrier, Nathaniel, I created my own preparatory ceremonies. I hiked into the flatirons and prayed for the group and for me. Those were powerful times. It was good to connect with nature and to set such good intentions for our trip. A couple of weeks later I put my belongings in storage and flew to Peru.

There were sixteen of us total. We spent the next couple of weeks with the most incredible indigenous healer from the Peruvian mountains, Don, and his companion and translator, Alfredo. These two were quite a pair. Don was old and wise and had led ceremonies and worked as a healer in his community for many years. Alfredo was young, a cute little man who played the siku, the traditional pan flute of the Andean people.

Our group travelled by bus all over Peru to sacred sites and held prayer ceremonies in each of them. After holding a group prayer circle and listening to some teachings we were often encouraged to hike into the sacred land and pray and meditate on our own. The beautiful sound of Alfredo's flute would eventually lure us back together and we would board the bus again and head off to another amazing spot. On the road, Don taught about the ways of the Peruvian people, the history of their spiritual beliefs and gave us messages of hope, truth and love. And Alfredo's endearing smile under his alpaca chullo hat was enough to brighten anyone's day.

At night, Don would perform healings. As someone who was on the path of becoming a healer, I watched him closely. On the bus we heard many stories about the healing practices of his people, but seeing it all in action was a different story. I noticed that as he went from person to person he would mirror their state, matching their tone. He would feel into the vibration and emotional state of a particular person, meet them at that place and perform healing.

One chilly night we were in a field with a fire roaring in the middle of the group. There was a woman who was wailing. She said she had back pain that she had endured for years and was very dramatic and emotional about it all. Don stepped in and began his healing. He worked with energy. It seemed as if he was having it out with spirits in another realm or something (of this I was never quite clear) and as he did this he was very dramatic and histrionic, matching her wails and emotional upset. I suppose he won the battle with the invisible spirits, as soon afterwards her crying quieted down and her back pain completely disappeared.

The following day I felt it was time to talk to Don about my healing. I went to him with an interpreter and explained the parasites I had in my brain. I gave him a brief synopsis of the all-encompassing experience I had lived through over the last years. I had told the story to so many doctors by that point that I was not emotional about it. He listened to the whole saga and looked at me and said plainly, "That is your story. It is only a story at this point. It is done. You will be fine." And that was that. I was curious about it. I thought he might single me out at the next fire and pull the worm demons out of my ears and make a big hoopla about it all, as the "story" was outrageous and strange, and it usually peaked the interest of every doctor I went to without fail. But with him, he matched my tone, he knew that it was a narrative, and knew that it was done.

And you know what? It was. That was the last time I was ever hospitalized for the parasites – not the last time I ever saw a doctor for it, but at least it was the last time I was admitted to the hospital. Whether it would have been "done" at that time anyway, without him saying that or not, I will never know. It was as if he healed me by saying those words and declaring it to the universe, to me, to the parasites, almost as a command – it was done.

Autumn was approaching and it was time for me to return to school, again. Yet instead of returning to naturopathic medical school, Spirit (and my intuition) was giving me a very clear message to go to chiropractic school instead and really master the art of hands-on medicine. But I was so resistant. My experience of chiropractors was that they were "back pain" doctors, people who "cracked your back." And I did not want to be a back pain doctor. It is a great service to get people out of back pain, but it absolutely did not light me up. I was more interested in true transformation, holistic healing and personal growth. But the universe would not let up with this clear message that I should go to chiropractic school. It came from every direction. I overheard conversations about people having amazing healing experiences with their chiropractor. People told me out of the blue that I would be a good chiropractor. I even saw a billboard about hands-on healing right when I was wondering what I should do. So finally, one day, I made a deal with God, and said, "Alright. Fine. I hear you. Chiropractic school. I will go, but when I get out I have to have a very different kind of practice than I have ever experienced from a chiropractor before."

The relentless tugging at my sleeves finally subsided and I felt a peace come over me. I moved back to the San Francisco area, reunited with my friends with such love, and started chiropractic college. My first day of school I was walking through the hallway and a young man came up to me exclaiming, "Hey, I know you! Don't you remember me? We hula-hooped on a grassy field at the High Sierra Music Festival years ago," and sure enough we had. We reconnected and started a friendship, one that is still strong. He introduced me to the chiropractic technique he was studying, a healing technique that blended quantum physics and transformation-based healing, with chiropractic medicine based on cutting edge research of western medicine and science. I could not believe what I was hearing when he told me about it. It was literally everything that I wanted, wrapped up in neat little package. I looked up at the sky, threw my arms up and laughed. At that point I knew my Saturn Return was officially over.

By this time a major shift started to occur. I began to get distance from the brain tumors and the havoc they had caused in my life, and I started to see, feel and experience how much they had taught me. I felt into myself and sensed a strength that was woven through my cells that wasn't there before. One of my greatest fears had occurred: being diagnosed with a life-threatening disease and being in and out of the hospital for years. And here I was. I had lived through it. I felt my resilience. I began to feel into that place inside that is unbreakable, untouchable. Despite the depression and anxiety I had lived through, all the seizures and the blindness, all the questioning and suffering, I found an essence in me that remained completely whole, unchanged by the worms, unchanged by the stress. An unbreakable part of me made of pure love. I had heard of that from teachers, and read about it, but now I felt it, experienced it and knew it deeply and completely in every cell of my body.

I also began to embody an understanding of what a healer was (to me). I started to understand that if I was going to be a true healer, I had to walk through my own darkness. I had to go through a major healing myself before trying to help others on their own unique healing path. I realized that I was called to be a "tour guide" for others to make their own journey through their challenges. And I could never have learned how to do that from a textbook or lectures. I thought back to those days in the African desert when I was constantly soul-searching for my path and purpose and I first felt a clear calling to be a healer in this world. I surrendered myself fully to that path. I offered myself to God, and said, "Take me. May I be your hands and feet in this world, may I be a vessel for Spirit, so you may work through me and spread love and healing energy into this world." And I truly thought that it meant going to medical school and becoming a doctor and healing people from diseases and infections and delivering babies. I was excited about that plan. But there was a different path in store for me.

It wasn't even three months after I had made that prayer of surrender in Africa that the blindness began. And the rest unfolded into a difficult and dark soupy mess of an experience that lasted for years. During that time I questioned the existence of God. I questioned Spirit's intentions for me, or if there even was such a thing, as I felt radically punished during most of that time. But I began to understand. Those worms were not in my brain just to be a hardship; they were there to shape me. They were there to create a fire to burn off or eat up any part of me that was no longer needed. They were there to whisper deep wisdom to me from the inside, to deliver my darkest hour so that I could make it through and truly help and empathize with others, only in the way that someone who has gone through it can.

I began to feel a deep sense of gratitude. For my life, for these nine creatures that were my teachers and the medium for me to develop so much strength and realize my true essence – unbreakable – the very definition of love.

Another thing that had been fired and polished throughout this experience was my belief in what I call "a beautiful spiral," our unique path that we walk, knowing that it is perfect, even when we cannot see it in the moment. Oh, believe me, I questioned this. So much. For so many years. And now that I was on the other side of it, I began to see that I was on my path, radically on it, all along. I struggled with the idea that I was supposed to be, and wanted to be, a healer. And to me, that meant completing a doctorate program and having some type of learned medicine that I could offer people. I struggled for so long feeling that it was my own illness that kept me from that. Each year that I deferred going to school I felt like I was a failure, and that some force, for some reason I could not figure out, was tying me down, holding me back. That it was keeping me from moving forward in my life, being able to have something of value to offer the world, and from having a successful career and family that I so longed for.

But it began to sink in on a deep level that living through and healing from Cerebral Cysticercosis *was* my offering. It was the very thing that started to shape me into a true healer, and not just a mechanic who could perform treatments learned from a book. I really understood how my illness was not keeping me from anything, but was the very thing I was seeking: true transformation, holistic healing and personal growth. A beautiful spiral that was being lived, danced and loved.

I completed my first year of chiropractic school and was ready for summer break. I found the environment challenging, being cooped up in windowless rooms all day with flickering fluorescent lights and stressed out students and the long days of lectures that started at 7:30 in the morning. I was ready for some sunshine and fresh air.

One of my best girlfriends asked me to join her at a yoga teacher training retreat in the beautiful Santa Cruz Mountains. I didn't have an interest in teaching yoga at that point, but I certainly wanted to learn more about it, and the program advertised that it was great for those who wanted to deepen their own practice even if they didn't want to teach. I agreed to go, packed up my tent and stretchy yoga pants and off I went to spend a month in meditation and yoga practice. It was an experience that my soul needed. After a year of being in drab classrooms memorizing a million pieces of information about biochemistry, microbiology and anatomy, I was now going to be immersed in practices that brought me into my body, surrounded by a beautiful clean lake and mountains filled with wildlife.

I returned from that experience feeling balanced, grounded, refreshed and connected. I was also feeling a deep longing for intimacy. It had been a while since I had dated anyone and I had spent that month in the mountains praying that a man would come into my life. I felt lonely and was ready to delve into a relationship. The week after I returned, a friend of mine from school called me up. He was a man in my class that I had not paid much attention to. He was my age, which was rare, as most of the students were much younger, and he confessed that he had developed a crush on me from the beginning of school. As we spoke on the phone I felt attraction and excitement build in my belly, and we soon had our first date. I invited him to my house and made him a delicious dinner of huge pieces of soft mozzarella cheese with basil and heirloom tomatoes, followed by fresh mushroom pasta in a cream sauce. They say that the way to a man's heart is through his stomach and I suppose that was true. It won him over quickly and we started seeing each other right away. We dated for the rest of the summer and we were falling in love, immersed in the swirls of a new relationship. As autumn approached, it was time for me to return to school. Gregory had stayed in school all summer, and as I was preparing to go back, he was feeling the need to take a break.

Gregory was an interesting man. There was so much more to him than met the eye. He had spent years living in India and had spent months on a crazy adventure through Mongolia on his bicycle, cycling all the way through Outer Mongolia to Pakistan and Nepal by himself, with nothing but a water filter, a small tent and a can opener. His sense of adventure matched my own and we started to dream big together. When he thought about taking a break from school that fall, he dreamed of returning to India, a place very dear to his heart. He asked me to go with him. At that point, we had only been dating for a few weeks. I laughed, and said, "Sure! I will go to India with you!" A big joke, a big dream! It was lighthearted and silly. But as time went on I could hear sincerity in his voice. He was asking me to go, not as a joke any more, but for real. He was asking me to be daring, to live big, dream big and go on a huge adventure with him. We would return to school in January. And I speak that language. The thought of going to India with him sounded romantic, wild, a bit irresponsible, fun and crazy. Right up my alley!

I found a sub-letter for my room and packed my backpack. We left hand in hand with excitement in our hearts. We arrived in Delhi after a terribly long journey and went to the rooftop restaurant at our hotel to eat our first meal. We asked the waiter to bring whatever he recommended and ate vegetable biryani while watching the sunset. And before we even woke up the next morning, we were already sick with bouts of diarrhea. We had tickets to board a train the next day and we spent the next night running from our sleeper car to the bathroom with watery diarrhea, trying to balance ourselves while the train swayed back and forth as we aimed for a hole in the floor which opened straight onto the train tracks.

We arrived in Dharamsala, a gorgeous mountain town that is home to the Dalai Lama, and had been home to Gregory years before. He knew of a good doctor there and we visited him right away. He gave us some medication, which helped me tremendously, but Gregory remained so sick that he could not leave the room. I revisited the doctor and told him about Gregory's condition, and he gave me some more medicine, and within a couple of days we were finally feeling ready to venture out of our room. Gregory knew that place well and he took me on beautiful, serene hikes into temples and good restaurants where we could order fresh food that helped heal our bellies. We marveled at the colors, smells and immensely different culture, and took in the majestic views of the mountains and beautiful architecture.

A few weeks after being there, I received an unexpected email announcing that the New Zealand College of Chiropractic was finally approved for American students to receive U.S. financial aid for the first time. I shared this news with Gregory and we began talking about what that could mean for us. I emailed the New Zealand College with a ton of questions and found out that the cost of attending their college was actually less than the one in California. We looked at their website for hours, gazing at the photographs of the new building that sat right in the middle of green fields with trails weaving through a beautiful park with streams and a small pond. Each classroom had walls lined with windows looking out over the grass and trees in a nice neighborhood, and they also had some top notch teachers there.

Both Gregory and I had spent years living overseas when we could, and we had both dreamed of one day visiting or living in New Zealand. We sat in contemplation, both separately and together, and decided to transfer to the New Zealand College of Chiropractic to take some classes. We applied to attend the college via fax from a tiny village in northern India. This process was a challenge as there was only one place with a fax machine that was only open a few hours a day – sometimes. We cut our trip to India short and returned home to pack our things and left for another journey.

Chapter 13

New Zealand

We arrived a couple of weeks before classes began and that gave us time to find an apartment and get a car. We rented a little apartment that was a five-minute walk from school. We rejoiced in not having to commute an hour back and forth to school on congested highways, and we loved seeing firsthand the sunny classrooms, and meeting the enthusiastic professors who spent hours putting together engaging and fascinating lectures. The students were from all over the world and we loved the international family that was forming. We spent the weekends exploring the stunning New Zealand coastline, and as we were both surfers, we invested in wetsuits and surfboards. Soon we had found our favorite spots to play. We counted our good fortune and were very glad we came.

New Zealand was a different world than what I had expected. The land vibrates with a clean, powerful energy that I have never witnessed before. It feels pristine; land that has been the least ravaged by humankind that I have ever seen. Jagged rocks rose right out of the ocean, clean seawater lapped at the land that felt pure and crisp like it all used to be. Rainforests, woodlands, glaciers and snow-peaked mountains right next to the surf. Rough hills surrounded sweet, sandy beaches – all within a short drive from one another. Gorgeous!

But the people didn't seem to match the physical land. Despite how vibrant and wild the flora was, the culture felt squashed to me. New Zealand seemed to be filled with nice people who would give you directions or help you with your car on the side of the road, but who would never open up about their dreams or fears or share what was really going on inside of themselves. And I felt darkness there, both in the native people and in the land. Sometimes it scared me. It felt like deep-seated anger and resentment stemming from the way the land and culture had been stripped from the Maori people, and from the natives before the Maori arrived. I witnessed a tremendous amount of effort to reintegrate and mend the rifts, but something stirred beneath the surface. It felt as if ghosts unable to rest roamed some parts of the beautiful land.

Nine months into our stay in New Zealand, the glow of new love that Gregory and I shared began to fade. Our relationship had been strained by the transition of moving in together, as well as moving across the world far away from friends and family. And what tends to happen in most relationships began in ours. The unhealthy patterns that we had adopted throughout our lives began to affect each other and feed into each other's triggers. Our home life became challenging and eventually tumultuous, and we eventually decided that it would be better if we separated.

My time at the college was coming to a close and I was heartbroken. I felt ungrounded and like I was shattered into pieces. I looked into my heart for a sign of what I needed to do. We were on track to return to California to finish chiropractic school. As it stood, Gregory and I would be in the same classes until we graduated, and I could not bear the idea of seeing him every day, distracting me from what I was supposed to be learning. I wanted space from him and some time to get centered in myself again.

So I decided to stay in New Zealand a little longer and spend some time in a personal retreat. This would allow time for Gregory to go back to school in California and take a quarter of classes before I returned so we would not have the same schedule any more. Little did I know how powerful my next move was going to be.

I followed my heart. I decided to move to my favorite surfing destination for a couple of months, a little town called Raglan, home to about 1,500 people with some of the best surfing and most beautiful beaches I have ever experienced, and I started my personal healing retreat.

When I arrived in Raglan, I went to the modest real estate office nestled in between a health food store and the coffee shop. In their front window they had a sign that advertised that they had short-term rentals available. I went inside and told them my situation. I was going to be in town for two months and needed a quiet place to stay, preferably close to the beach. The woman apologized and said, "Oh, I am so sorry. We should have taken that sign down a long time ago. We don't handle those any more. Sorry."

When I began to walk away, a woman suddenly exclaimed from the back, "Wait! I have the perfect thing! I have a friend with a little garden apartment in the bottom of her house. I think you two would love each other! This is perfect!" She said that I could drive by and see the location and the front of the house, and see if I was interested. I drove down the street and found the house easily. It was close to the beach and sat on a rolling hill with a huge yard in the back with trees and flowers, and there was a fence that went across the front of the house with a large metal gate that spanned the driveway. I sat and stared in amazement at the artwork on the gate. It had a metal sculpture on it with swirls and spirals that looked exactly like the tattoo that covers my left arm. It couldn't have been a better match. I immediately knew, before even seeing the inside of the place or meeting this woman, that it was the right place for me.

The next day I met a woman named Elisha, the owner of the house, and we hit it off right away. She was a homeopath, counselor and mother of three young adults. She was in a period of her life in which she was retired from practice and going through a healing process herself, as was I, and it seemed that as I was going to be doing a personal retreat downstairs, she was going through a similar process upstairs. We felt like family right away and I decided to move in. I drove back to Auckland to get the rest of my bags and visit my friends one more time, and by the time I returned to Raglan my new home was ready for me to move in, and so my retreat began.

The downstairs was small but charming, with windows that spanned one whole wall that looked over their backyard. I spent the first day there journaling and getting clear on what I wanted my time there to be like. I knew I wanted to cleanse, to get reconnected to myself, to replenish and renew, and holistically heal myself. I decided to do a whole-foods cleanse and committed to eating a diet full of vegetables, fruit, fish, nuts, seeds and raw oils for two months. I cut out caffeine, sugar, wheat, processed foods, and other kinds of meat and eggs. I also wrote a list of daily practices that I wanted to do there, and posted them on the wall. The list looked something like this:

Take morning temperature
Write in my dream journal
Herbal detox tea
Take vitamins and supplements
Meditation and breathing exercises
Surf or exercise and stretch
Dry brush my skin
Write my life story: 1,500 words a day

I wanted to take my temperature in the morning each day to start keeping track of my menstrual cycle, something I had always wanted to do and had never made the time for. I had never been in touch with my cycle my whole life and I wanted to know my body in that way. The dream journal was an exercise that I had never done either. Each morning when I woke and after putting the thermometer in my mouth, I would write as much as I could remember about my dreams and re-read my entries as the days and weeks went by. I ended up learning a lot about how my dreams would repeat themselves in different ways, revealing themes of what my subconscious mind was working on. The meditation and breathing exercises were the ones I learned at the yoga teacher training. I kept up the practices during the summer following the training, but when I went traveling to India and made the move to New Zealand, the practices went by the wayside, especially since Gregory did not do them as well. I knew I felt centered, calm and grounded when I did them, and I wanted to bring those practices back into my life.

The idea of writing my life story came from a friend of mine who participated in National Novel Writing Month each year. He told me that he would get together with folks in his area who were also writing a novel, and the goal was to write a whole book in a month. They had a goal of writing 1,500 words a day, and if they felt inspired they would write more than that, but they didn't have to. At the end of the month, they would have written an entire novel. People had always told me that I should write my life story. Between my crazy travels and the experience with the brain tumors it seemed that my story was wild, unique and full of life lessons. I never felt that I had the time, or the drive. But now it seemed appropriate.

So I started writing. I was writing more as a cathartic experience rather than writing for anyone else to read it. Alas, I never thought I would share it with anyone. But the whole process became a huge part of my cleanse. It turned out that writing about the brain tumors and the aftermath of that was amazingly healing for me. I had journaled over the years, but I had never put things together in a clear and concise way. I had never laid out the journey from start to finish, nor pondered what each stage had taught me. I felt like I was pulling on something that was trapped in my body and psyche and that I was finally getting it out of me, making sense of it and learning about myself in a whole new way. It became one of the most powerful parts of my cleanse.

Some days writing 1,500 words was like pulling teeth. I struggled to get them out at all, and as soon as I hit the 1,500 word mark I would stop mid-sentence and leave my computer frustrated, yet proud of myself for completing my goal for the day. Sometimes I sat and wrote for ten hours straight and things just flowed. And I never knew what kind of day it was going to be until I started writing. It helped that I had many strings of my story going at once. Sometimes I would sit and struggle with how to finish part of a thread I was working on, and would remember that I also had another piece of my story unfinished in a different section of the book, and when I switched to that part of my story it would flow easily and prolifically. The next day I would return to the original one I was working on and for whatever reason, that day I could write about it without a problem. By the time I left, I had written about my whole life up to that point. I had surpassed my goal of writing 50,000 words, and had been blessed with an unexpected journey of a cathartic cleanse using words as a medium.

Another avenue for healing that was unexpected for me was my relationship with Elisha and her family. Elisha was a wise woman and had worked in service as a healer to many, and I was fortunate to have her help as I navigated my journey healing from my relationship with Gregory, as well as processing the things coming up during my writing process about the rest of my life.

I stayed disciplined with the cleanse and completed my daily practice goals 100 percent. I was accountable to nobody but myself, though it was hard at times to keep to the schedule. It was hard to keep eating broccoli when I wanted a hamburger. It was hard to keep writing each day when I didn't feel inspired. It was even harder to drink that detox tea every day when I didn't feel like it – but I did. I went surfing almost every day, even when I didn't feel like putting on my soggy wetsuit and venturing out into the sometimes choppy sea and yet, by the time I left that sweet little apartment, I felt replenished, renewed and reconnected to myself, exactly what I had wanted for myself at that time.

And I had written my life story. I had recorded my incredible journey, including the years of suffering and the challenges that having the worms in my brain had put me through. I had not only survived, but was well on my way to becoming the doctor I had dreamed of becoming. Writing the book meant closure.

The suffering was behind me now.

I truly felt healthy and whole, strong and independent, and ready to return to the U.S. once more to finish my training as a doctor of chiropractic medicine and take my place as a healer in service to others.

I was both a survivor and a healer. And I felt incredibly blessed. The road ahead seemed clear and bright.

This time – yes!

Part Two

Chapter 14

Violated

Breathe.
Must breathe.
One minute tucked in bed.
The next…

April 23, 2009. It's a Thursday.

I just moved back to the United States after studying at the New Zealand College of Chiropractic and I am now in my third year of chiropractic college. I finish my day at the school around 4 p.m. and go to the DMV to register my newly purchased car. After waiting some time in a long line, I realize that I have left my wallet at the college and have no way to pay for my registration. Frustrated at my forgetfulness, I drive to my new little cottage only to find my home feeling totally "off." I have only lived there for three weeks but things were already organized and settled in. Yet I feel there is something wrong there today.

I can't put my finger on it. I look in the mirror and feel that something is off there too. Everything just feels strange.

I go to the small kitchen and make a smoothie, trying to calm down by making myself a healthy treat. But I leave the metal spoon in the blender by accident, and when I turn it on it makes a horrible jangly noise that seems to echo throughout the small house and make things feel even worse. This strange feeling of "off-ness" is all-pervasive; I don't know what to do. So I decide to take action. Change things. I resolve to paint my kitchen a new color. Right then and there. And dye my hair a new color. See if that makes things feel better.

I just bought my car the week before and haggled the man down from the price he was asking, so I have two hundred-dollar bills left over from that purchase. I keep them in a little wooden box next to my bed for safekeeping. Since my wallet is at school, I open the little decorative box and grab one of the bills and leave. After a quick visit to Home Depot for some paint and the drug store for hair color, I return home and begin changing colors. As the color sets in my hair, I begin painting my kitchen. Mind you, I live in a 400-square-foot studio so my "kitchen" is really just one wall with a window, and a stove and sink up against it. So painting my kitchen is not a substantial project, to say the least.

The quick transformation is making me feel better. After the first coat of paint is on, it's getting late and the color needs to be washed out of my hair. I have classes at 7:30 the next morning and I need to get into bed. I take a long shower and as I get out to dry I hear something out in the yard, through the small window near the shower. I look out into the darkness but I can see nothing. I live on a property with four dogs and they are always out and about, plus there are always squirrels and other creatures around so I dismiss it and put on my pajamas. Considering it has been a weird day, I put on my favorite t-shirt, my soft, striped pajama bottoms that are loose and comfortable, and go to bed.

I am reading a great book, a gift from a friend called *Black Elk Speaks*. The little lamp next to my bed creates a warm glow as I read, and within a few minutes I'm absorbed in the story of Black Elk. He was a Native American who was born into a troubled time in Indian history. He had visions as a child, which meant to his tribe that he was a healer, a shamanistic-type leader. During his adolescence, the "white man" arrived and started taking the land from the Indians and killing them as they battled to keep it. He lived to tell the horrific tale and this book is his first-hand account of this terrible part of our history.

I'm absorbed in my book.

My front door flies open.

Immediately I think this must be my new boyfriend. He has a tiger spirit and loves to hide behind corners or in the closet and jump out and scare me. We decided to spend tonight apart, but I guess he just can't bear to be apart from me and he's come over to surprise me!

But after that split second of a thought, I see the face of a man and he's not my boyfriend. My fair-skinned blue-eyed blond boyfriend.

This is a huge African American man with his dark hoodie cinched around his face so only his wild eyes are showing.

In this moment I realize that he is an intruder – and I'm in serious trouble.

My body flushes with fear and panic. I don't have a chance to move before he reaches me.

He runs straight to my bed – and in a tiny 400-square-foot studio it happens in a flash. Yet my brain seems to work in slow motion. In the flash of time it takes him to come in the door and get to my bed, I think, 'Oh, it's my boyfriend. He loves to play these games. Wait a second, that's not him. Who's that? I don't know him. What the fuck? This is wrong! What do I do?'

Before I know it he is upon me and reaches right for my throat. He starts strangling me. He is big and he is on top of me with all his weight directed through his hands right onto my throat and I cannot breathe.

I struggle to get out from underneath him and fight to get his hands off my throat. But I'm not strong enough to do either. Within seconds he keeps his right hand pressed hard on my throat and reaches with his left hand to the wall behind the covers. He pulls the plug from the wall and it goes completely dark.

I can't see him anymore but I can feel his hands on my throat and I cannot breathe. At all.

He begins talking. He leans down to my ear and says quickly, quietly, "Stop struggling or I will kill you. I am going to take all your money." He keeps saying these words over and over, in a horrible whisper while his hands cut off my breath.

My mind seems to be clear somehow. All I can think is "This is not right. How can I get out of this? What can I do? This is not right." But all I can do is try to breathe. I struggle against him with all my might, unsuccessfully.

He just keeps saying over and over again, "Stop struggling or I will kill you. I am going to take all your money. Do you understand? I am going to take all your money. Stop moving or I will kill you!"

Finally, it starts to sink in that I am in a losing battle, and that perhaps if I stop fighting against him he might take all my money, which I don't care about, and let me go. So I drop my hands.

My eyes are wildly open. My body is more awake than it has ever been, as adrenaline and fear rush through my whole system.

He releases my throat and asks me where my money is.

I'm honest with him. I tell him with a raspy voice that my wallet is at school, but I have a $100 dollar bill in the little box next to my bed, and some more in a backpack against the wall – the change from the paint and hair color earlier in the evening. Although that's the truth, I'm afraid he will not believe that my wallet is at school. I fear he's going to hurt me again but he doesn't. He never even questions it. But instead of taking the money and leaving, he pushes down on my throat again. Even harder.

He cuts off my air completely for so long I know I am going to die. I cannot breathe in or out for so long that I see stars and white light all around me. I am terrified that if I lose consciousness he will have his way with my body and I won't be able to do anything about it.

I do not want that to happen – and I do not want to die.

I struggle with all my might to stay conscious. But I feel fear to the core of my being as my entire body tightens and my bowels let loose in my pants.

Then suddenly, I can breathe. Just a little. Just enough to take in a little air. I hear the sound so clearly. The sound of me trying to get air into my body. It sounds so sick, so otherworldly and terrible.

He keeps one hand on my throat, and the other hand reaches up and grabs my t-shirt. In one pull he rips my shirt right off my body. In this moment I know he is there to do more than just take my money.

This is my greatest fear.

I had nightmares as a child of men coming into my house raping my mother or me. I developed strategies when I was little about where I would hide my small body and what I would do to save my mom if those men ever broke in.

And now it is actually happening. I know I have to get out of here. My brain is in overdrive trying to problem-solve. What can I do? What can I do?

In that moment I have an idea. I reach up and grab his balls and squeeze with all my might.

It works! He topples over in pain and I wiggle my way out from under him. I race for the door. But halfway across the small room he tackles me from behind. We both fall to the floor knocking over a bar stool on the way down. I am face down on a hard floor with him on my back.

He reaches his hands around my face and I bite his thumb. With my teeth locked down on his thumb he bends down and starts biting the back of my head at the top of my skull. We stay this way, neither one of us letting go. I feel his teeth sinking into the skin on the back of my skull. But I will not let go.

Then suddenly he lets go of my head with his teeth, grabs the back of my hair with his hand and smashes my forehead into the hard floor. The blow to my head causes me to release my bite hold. I am stunned. He then reaches around my throat with his forearm and gets me in a choke hold.

Again, I cannot breathe. At all.

I am now on the bed being strangled again. (It's strange – I do not remember losing consciousness, nor do I remember being moved from face down on the floor to back onto the bed and on my back, but here I am.) My hands are on his wrists and forearms trying to lift them, unsuccessfully, off my throat so I can breath.

With one hand on my throat, he now pulls my pajama bottoms off with the other hand. He realizes I have soiled my pants, and starts wiping my butt with my pants to clean it off. He then grabs the sheets, the blanket, anything he can find to wipe the shit off me. This whole time I struggle to lift his big hand off my throat. His entire weight bears down on me and my attempts are futile, but at times I lift his hand just enough to suck a small breath. And again, there is that sound. The sound of the sides of my throat flapping together as so little air is forced through a tiny squished space.

Then – the smell. The smell of fear and adrenaline so thick in that small house. I cannot describe that smell other than it is sweet – sickly sweet, mixed with sweat and now with the smell of shit. So pungent as he wipes me and throws the sheets and blankets to the side. It fills the room.

I am completely filled with fear, my sympathetic nervous system fully engages and my brain is completely awake despite the lack of oxygen and physical violence, thinking, thinking, thinking how to get out of there, how I can get away from this man and

I NEED TO BREATHE RIGHT NOW!!!

My pants are off. I know he is going to rape me.

He is between my legs and begins to take his pants down.

He pulls my left leg open to the side with his free hand and begins to put himself inside me – his left hand never leaves my throat. The rape is not too painful between my legs, at least I don't think so, but I can feel what is going on. All my attention is focused on my throat and

HIS HAND. LIFT HIS GODDAMNED HAND OFF MY THROAT SO I CAN STAY ALIVE!!!

The actual rape doesn't seem to take long, but I don't have any sense of how much time is passing. I suppose he ejaculates. I am not sure. But after a while he stops.

And he lets go of my throat. Finally.

And he gets off of me.

Naked, I twist and writhe on the bed, trying to breath through a crushed throat. I think to myself at least it is over. There is nothing else he can do now.

I can't remember his next words exactly, but it is clear he is spurting racial hatred at me while he pulls his pants back up, blaming me for how white people have treated black people!

I shake my head and gasp. This is enough to make him stop his ranting and growl, "What?"

I hiss through my torn throat: "It's ironic you choose me! I am not a racist woman. I lived in Africa as a Peace Corps Volunteer, and even now I am in school to be a chiropractor… I am here to serve you… I am here to serve *you*! It's so ironic you choose me to do this to!"

He ignores me.

He looks around my house for things to steal. He goes to the little box next to my bed and takes the hundred-dollar bill. He goes to the backpack and rummages through it looking for money and other things to take. He grabs some other stuff from around the house. I can't see what he takes, it is dark and I am on the bed focusing on getting my breath back. I'm in pain, shock and barely conscious.

He then turns to me and says, "I have a gun in my pocket. I am going to shoot you and kill you if you move. I will be watching you through your window. You lay here for ten minutes and give me time to get away. If you move, I will kill you."

Then he runs out the door into the darkness.

Chapter 15

Invasive Inspection

I could hear the gate click behind him and I knew he was no longer watching me at that point. I knew he was running as fast as he could to get away from this place. I first crawled to my bedside table – I was lying nearly upside down on the bed at that point – and reached for my water glass. My throat was so ripped and sore I could barely breathe even though he was not touching me any more. The water seemed to help tremendously.

I got up, sore and foggy and terrified. I put on some clothes slowly and began looking for my phone. I couldn't find it. I looked everywhere. I never saw that man's face. I knew I would never be able to identify him at all, and so I wasn't going to call the police. I wanted to call my boyfriend. And lie in his arms and be comforted.

But I searched and searched and couldn't find that damned phone. Furniture was turned over and things were everywhere, but I could not find the phone in the mess.

Finally, I stumbled through the yard to my landlord's house on the front of the property. I struggled to get up the steps as I was light-headed and very weak, staggered through their door and went inside. I woke up my landlord, who was asleep in front of the TV and told him I had just been raped. It was as if he couldn't understand me. I strained out the words, "A man just broke into my house and raped me. I need help. I can't find my phone." At that point I collapsed on his couch and what I had told him began to sink in and he started freaking out. "Oh my God.

Oh my God, Oh my God. Margaret, wake up!" The commotion roused his wife and she came out of her bedroom. He told her what happened, in fragments, as he was clearly in shock. She started yelling and wailing and called the police immediately.

"What happened? What happened?" they kept asking. I could barely speak my throat was so sore, and they were talking so loud, and the dogs were barking too, because of the commotion. I didn't get much of an explanation out, but within a few minutes a policeman was there.

As soon as he entered the dark room, he came right to me and put a bright flashlight in my eyes. "What is your name? Tell me what happened," he demanded. I was weak and the light was so blinding. I squinted and cowered from the light, barely able to answer his questions.

The whole scene was about as un-nurturing as you can get, and all I wanted to do was lie in my man's arms and be caressed, hugged and comforted. I wanted to escape from this madness and crawl into a safe, loving haven. Where was that goddamned phone? But there I was, in that crazy, messy living room with a cop's flashlight right in my eyes and my landlords screaming in fear.

An ambulance arrived soon afterwards, and I was strapped into a gurney and loaded into the back. I know it was "for my safety" but I hated being strapped to the gurney. It made me feel like they thought I was a crazy person again and needed to be confined in a straightjacket-sort-of contraption. I felt like the tables were turned in a strange way, and I was the criminal being carted off to be punished. The officer got into the ambulance with me. He asked me all sorts of questions during the ride and took notes. I tried to convey the story through my very painful throat.

It was during that ride that I had a great realization. All of a sudden I felt space around me and sensed the infinite expanse of the universe. I felt time in each direction, both into the past and into the future, and things became quiet despite the cop talking and the ambulance siren screaming above my head.

And a message came to my consciousness. Not in a voice, but a knowing. I was meant to help women through this in the future. I had been called to be a healer a long time ago, and I was supposed to help women heal from experiences like this, to understand them and give compassion in a way that only a woman who has gone through it can understand.

That message, that understanding, was clear to me that night. And I had no idea at the time but that outlook, that message saved my life.

Let me just say that after a woman is raped she needs to be nurtured. She needs to be in a soft, supportive environment and made as comfortable as possible. She really needs a huge hug. This is the opposite of what I experienced that night. I was fed into a system that had not been thought through – at all. Someone needs to think about it and develop different protocols.

When we finally arrived at the hospital, I was rolled out of the ambulance strapped to the gurney and taken to a hallway right by the doors leading into the emergency room. It was drafty, chaotic and a big feng shui disaster. People were constantly walking by, squeezing by. Other patients were being rolled in on gurneys. Some were crazy and were rambling disturbing nonsense. Some were homeless and dirty, some bloody and in shock. The mere experience of sitting in that hallway under blaring fluorescent lights was terrible in itself, much less for someone who had just gone through what I had.

I was in shock, and the scene I was witnessing was disturbing to the core.

Finally, after what felt like hours, I was taken to a room to wait for a physical exam that I was supposed to have, some sort of inspection.

The police officer came with me and we were taken to a drab, messy room with a chair, an examining table with a flimsy blanket, a desk with a computer, and boxes stacked on it, under it and all over the floor. It was disorganized and seemed like some sort of storage room, a dumping zone.

And I sat in there under glaring lights in the ugly chaos of that room for hours. Hours.

Yes, nice protocol, people.

All I wanted was my boyfriend.

I wanted to be held.

I wanted to disappear in his arms and feel safe, warm, loved and taken care of. But my cell phone was gone and I did not know anyone's number by memory.

I didn't even know my own mama's number.

I convinced the officer to use the computer to get online so I could check my email. I began searching frantically through my messages looking for my boyfriend, Trevor's, number.

I couldn't find it.

I needed someone.

After a while I just started looking for anyone's number.

I came across a friend's message with his phone number and called him.

By that point it was around three in the morning.

He answered, thank God, and listened to my story with concern and support.

He said he would try to get Trevor's number for me, and said he would be down at the hospital as soon as he could.

He actually called his girlfriend as well, another friend of mine, and they arrived within about half an hour.

I can't imagine what it was like for them walking in to see me. My hair had the color of a cheap hair dye several shades darker than what it was the day before. It was pulled into a bun before the attack, but in the struggle the bun came undone with all my squirming around, so my hair was sticking out wildly in every direction. My lips were totally blue from the prolonged lack of oxygen, while the rest of my face was still ashen white. I had dark circles under my eyes from exhaustion and fright. I am sure my face was contorted with tension. Although the darkest bruises didn't show up fully for another couple of days, my neck was all red and the skin was ripped. They looked terrified when they saw me, but they tried to be supportive and told me that my boyfriend was on his way. A relief.

About that time, two women that I did not know came in. After introducing themselves, one of the women said, "We're volunteers. We are survivors of rape ourselves. A long time ago, we sat in the hospital one night just like you are doing. We are here simply to support you, sit with you and help you tonight."

They were on call as volunteers and had come from their homes. At that point my friends were there, and shortly afterwards, my boyfriend too. I wanted to be with familiar faces, so I thanked them profusely and let them know I would be better off being with the people I knew and loved. They made sure I was all right with that decision and then gave me a packet of information in case I needed any support in the future.

Wow. How amazing that women would volunteer to get up in the middle of the night to go and sit with other women who had gone through this. I am still in awe of that. That is one protocol that *has* been thought through. But not by the hospital – by the rape support group. Thank God for them.

I sat in that messy room with Trevor for another hour. I tried to relay the story despite my exhaustion and raspy throat, but mostly I just wanted to be in his arms.

Finally, a nurse came in and wheeled me to another room to see a physician's assistant for a physical exam. My friends left but Trevor stayed with me, and I was given a gown to put on.

There was some sort of "rape kit" they use when a woman comes in after an assault, and the physician's assistant was a very nice woman. But talk about another very un-nurturing, traumatic experience – especially for someone who has just experienced a violent rape.

I was told to take my pants off and lie on my back, spread my legs wide and put my feet up in stirrups. The room was cold and there was a terrible glaring light above me.

I felt so exposed – emotionally it was so difficult to spread my legs like that. The P.A. put on gloves and inspected my vagina and outer genital area. She put a speculum inside me and looked at my skin with some sort of black light. She told me that there were tears in my skin and took many swabs from deep inside of me hoping to get sperm and fluids from the attacker.

She took photographs of my vagina for evidence.

And finally, after what felt like an eternity of being uncomfortably poked and prodded, I was able to close my legs and sit up.

She inspected the inside of my throat, which was completely covered with small red sores. Tissue damage from being choked, she explained. I had bitten my tongue very badly and there was a big chunk missing from the side of it.

She recorded and took pictures of everything, and finally left me with a pair of hospital-issued underwear and sweat pants to put on, as they took my favorite pair of jeans as evidence, in case there was any residual fluid on it.

On an emotional level, a woman who has just been raped needs *loving* touch.

To open my legs like that and be poked and prodded felt like another violation.

There was no healing offered at the hospital on any level.

Just an invasive inspection.

It seemed so ironic.

I felt like a bug under a microscope. All my private parts turned under a bright harsh light, exposed in a blunt way just when I was feeling the most tender in my entire life.

I understand that the police will need evidence for a court case, but the victim needs to be treated like a human being – one who has just gone through one of the most terrifying, awful experiences there is on this earth. Somewhere in our "system," especially in a hospital, there needs to be some expression of true compassion and healing offered.

I finally left the hospital with Trevor, and we were told to go to the police station. We followed the officer to the station where I was taken to small room with a tape recorder and two detectives who asked me to tell my story. They inquired about every detail.

They kept asking me what I could remember about him so they could have something to go on as far as finding him.

I could tell them nothing.

Because he had his hoodie cinched closed, I never even saw his face other than his eyes and a small part of his nose, and even that was just for a split second.

I could not even remember what color clothes he was wearing. He pulled the cord to the light when he first came in so I only saw him for a few seconds, and my mind was totally preoccupied with who he was and how to get out of there, rather than taking note of the color of his jeans and tennis shoes.

I knew he would have a bite mark on his left thumb from where I bit him, but other than that I would not be able to recognize him even if he was in front of me.

They were thorough with their questioning, and seemed totally willing to help in any way they could. I told them everything that I knew, but I felt hopeless. Without being able to visually identify him, I felt there was no way he would ever be found. Even if I could identify him, how would they ever find him?

Chapter 16

Unlocked

My landlords had lived on that property for many years and told me they had never locked their doors. They had four large dogs that were free to roam in and out of their house with the doors left wide open, and they had never had any problems. The little cottage that I moved into sat on the back of their large property and was surrounded by gardens, fruit trees and green fields. It was a short bike ride away from the chiropractic college I attended, and although it was tiny it had everything I needed. I loved it.

Shortly after I moved in, I met my boyfriend Trevor, who lived in a very similar cottage down the street from me. And oddly enough, he also said he never locked his doors either. He had lived there for years and he liked to live that way – open and trusting. I had also just moved back to the U.S. from a tiny coastal town in New Zealand, where it seemed that hardly anyone locked their doors to their homes or their cars.

So one day I decided to live a little differently. I made a conscious decision, even though it scared me, that I was going to start leaving my doors unlocked. I chose to trust humanity. I called my mom one day and told her that I started leaving my door unlocked, that I wanted to trust in that way. She tried to dissuade me, being the protective mom that she is, but I rolled my eyes, thinking, "God, Mom, you are so old school. You will never understand." I wanted to listen to my trust, not my fears, so that night when the rapist broke into my home, my door was unlocked. I had just started leaving it open earlier that week.

I got home from the police station when the sun was already high in the sky. I had been up all night long and was exhausted, but when we arrived at Trevor's house I could not sleep.

I was afraid.

I was not sure how long that man had been watching me through my window. Since he knew where the plug was that led to the lamp, I wondered if he had been in my house when I was away, since my doors were unlocked, planning the rape and scouting it all out. I was afraid that the rapist had seen Trevor's truck at my house and somehow figured out where he lived or followed him home one day. Trevor's little cottage was in the middle of a large yard, and his bathroom was across the lawn in a little building all on its own, almost like a little outhouse but with plumbing. When I went over to the little building to use the bathroom, I was terrified that that man was hiding behind the shower curtain or was watching me from the yard. My nervous system was still totally in fight-or-flight mode and I was scared out of my wits, reacting to every sound thinking someone was out there. Would he stalk me? Was he angry that I had gone to the police? Did he have a gun after all? Was he watching me through Trevor's window? Would he shoot me?

I told Trevor all about my fears. He tried to comfort me and offered some kava kava root extract to calm me down, which I accepted. And after a while I fell into a deep sleep. However, I only slept for two or three hours and then I was awake again, terrified. Trevor and I spoke about what to do next. We decided to get out of town, go into the mountains. I wanted to be away from his house, this whole city, and go to some place to be in nature where I knew I would be safe.

But first I wanted to see a healer. There was a woman whose chiropractic practice is rooted in the vitalistic philosophy of healing that I too had embraced: the idea that throughout life, our physical and emotional beings integrate all of our experiences. When we have an experience that is too much for us to integrate in the moment our body stores it inside. The body adapts and compensates by storing that information as tension in the body, with the lessons of that experience held within it. The healing work she offered was done with the intention of helping people integrate experiences that were stored in the body, thus moving the body back towards a place of optimal alignment and less tension. And I was definitely not able to integrate what I had just gone through. I could feel my body buzzing with energy and could already feel the tension from the physical injuries as well as my emotional state. I wanted to get some work from her to help dissipate the buzz and assimilate what I could.

When I entered her office I told her what had happened. I also told her of my realization that I was supposed to help women in the future, and that I needed to heal from this in the best possible way so I could be a positive example to share with others what had worked for me (this was less than twenty-four hours after the assault). After an amazing session, she told me to have patience. She told me this healing process would take a long time, and although she appreciated my willingness to start the process of healing, I needed to be very gentle with myself and cultivate patience with the process. This was very good guidance, and thus my healing journey began with a fierce focus on my healing blended with a sweet-tempered, nurturing heart.

Trevor and I headed up into the mountains. During the journey he suggested that we build a sweat lodge. I readily accepted, knowing how healing and powerful they had been for me in the past. We arrived, hefted our backpacks onto our backs and hiked a winding trail through the tall forest down to a beautiful stream and started to set up camp. Trevor was in his element outdoors and he was on a mission. He gathered fallen wood quickly, built a fire and put rocks in the center to heat them up. We cut flexible branches for the lodge and draped towels and blankets from his truck over the dome. I brought together soft fern leaves, small flowers and candles we had brought and infused the inside of the lodge with a sweet femininity that I had never experienced with Nathaniel's lodges, but somehow here it felt right. When we were ready, Trevor brought in the hot rocks one by one. The small lodge was gorgeous and glowing from the candles and smoldering rocks, and slowly the heat intensified with each stone that was brought in.

That night I felt like I cleansed so much out of my body. I prayed for healing, I gave up the experience to Spirit, to service, to love. I prayed for the man who raped me. I prayed for the police who were searching for him. I prayed for myself and for wisdom how to navigate this part of my path. It was powerful and probably the best thing in the world I could have done that night.

We returned to the city late Monday night. But as we got closer, I felt the same terror creep up in me – the rapist was there, around every corner.

Tuesday morning, Trevor got up to go to school, as he was studying at the same chiropractic college. I did not want to be alone and didn't know what else to do, so I went to school too.

I went straight to the Dean's office and told them what had happened to me. At that point I realized what a big mistake it was for me to have told the rapist that I was in chiropractic school. The chiropractic college I went to was the only one in town.

So that morning when I was on campus, I was scared stiff that he was going to find me there. Each time I went into the bathroom I looked into every stall before I allowed myself into one to pee.

It was living a nightmare.

That afternoon a miracle occurred. I got a call on Trevor's phone, which I had in case the police called. The team of officers working on my case asked me to come to the station right away.

They said they had him.

They had just caught the man who raped me and they needed me to come down to hear the rest of the story.

When Trevor and I arrived, the whole team of officers was so excited they could hardly sit down. Over the weekend when I was up in the mountains they had confirmed that the rapist had stolen my cell phone. He used it to call a couple of people the night he left my house, which in the end led to his arrest. They said he was smart about it and didn't leave the phone on long enough for them to use GPS to track it, so they were getting frustrated. But they did track down the two numbers that he had dialed. They immediately found the address of the first number and asked for the owner of the phone. The older woman said it belonged to her son who was at work. She gave them his office address and off they went. When they found the man, he was surprised to see the officers and said he would gladly answer their questions. The cops were actually laughing as they told me this part of the story.

They said this guy was an older man; a bus driver who transported mentally handicapped kids to school and on field trips. They explained to him that someone had raped a woman, stolen her phone and then dialed his number. They needed to know how he was connected to the rapist and what he had said on the phone. His boss overheard this conversation and started to shout that this guy was fired – right on the spot. Then the man said that he remembered answering the phone at the time the cops described, but that the person hung up. The cops called the phone company to confirm this, and lo and behold, the call lasted all of two seconds.

Directly after, another call was made from the phone that lasted for over ten minutes. The second number was one digit off from the first and it became clear that the first call was a misdial. The man's boss gave him his job back, and the police apologized and left.

The detectives then went to find the recipient of the second phone call. The household consisted of a teenage girl and her parents. The girl had answered the door, and immediately knew what the police were asking about. She agreed to go to the police station for questioning. She told them that her friend, the rapist, called her the night of the assault and then came over to her house. He told her, in some detail, what he had done, including the rape. He showed her the money and other objects that he had stolen, and showed her my phone. The police said that her description of everything matched my own, including the denomination of the bills I reported. She even described my phone in great detail. She told the police that she did not agree with what he did, and that she was willing to help them, even though this man was her friend. At that moment, her cell phone rang. It was a mutual friend of hers and the rapist's, so the police told her to answer it. After talking with him for a minute or so she covered the mouthpiece and whispered to the police that he was sitting next to the man they wanted. The police told her to keep her friend on the phone as long as possible while they used GPS to track him.

Within a couple of minutes they had a ground crew surrounding the men. They were sitting in an old abandoned car with two other buddies, and when the cops showed up everyone in the car ran away except the man who raped me. He knew they were after him and he just stayed there stunned for a second. However, he soon freaked out and started to run as well. The police chased him, then tasered him. He struggled to get away, so eventually they had to send the dogs after him. They got him though, and he was in custody. The detectives had worked twenty-seven hours straight and had spent the entire night interrogating him. They said that my cell phone was in his pocket when they arrested him, and he admitted to everything. He gave them details of my house that no one else would know unless they had been in there. They knew it was him for sure.

I was amazed.

I had not hoped for this, especially considering I could not identify him. But it turned out that they were able to get hairs and skin cells from my apartment for DNA matching, they had a witness (the young girl) to whom he had told everything, he gave a recorded full confession, and my phone was in his pocket. It was about as tight a case as you could get.

The detectives were smiling and giving each other high fives. You could see it in their faces that they were totally exhausted but also elated. They said that to have this kind of closure for a case was like winning the Super Bowl. Unfortunately it didn't happen nearly as often as they would like so when it did happen, it made everything else worth it and they were unbelievably happy to have served me in this way. They worked so hard over the weekend, and worked every angle trying to get this man. The miracle of that phone call to the teenage girl while she was being questioned was such amazing synchronicity I could barely believe it.

After our meeting, the officers finally went home to see their families and sleep. I sat in awe of the nature of their work that focused on the darkest spectrum of humanity, their commitment and how they put themselves in great danger day after day. I will never look at members of the police force the same way. I am ever grateful for those men.

The next day the cops showed me the phone that was found in the suspect's pocket so I could verify that it was mine. My belly swirled with emotion when I saw it. It was my phone all right.

He really was the one.

Hot damn.

I was still in such a tender place despite the fact that the rapist was caught. I was shaken up, exhausted, bruised, sore and still in shock. I had an idea to have a women's circle, pulling together my closest friends to have a healing ceremony for me. The very thought of this felt like salve to my wounded body and heart. I sent an email with a brief description of what had happened to me and asked my sisters to come together to support and pray for me. I asked them to bring whatever they felt would help me and asked an older friend, sweet Janna, to facilitate it. She readily agreed and another friend offered her beautiful home to host the gathering.

About a week after the rape, my dear friends came together for a beautiful ceremony that made me feel held and healed. Many of these women were from different times and places in my life and did not know each other, but they all brought their love and support, and on that night we became a tight circle of sisters. My friends showed me the different things they brought for the altar, and one by one they placed the special objects in the center of the circle on a gorgeous piece of fabric laid down by our hostess. Janna opened the circle, and they all offered up prayers for me, one by one.

As we finished they gathered around me on the bed. I lay back in Janna's arms and one of the women asked if it was OK if they all put their hands on me. I actually longed for it. So they placed their feminine healing hands on me while they asked me to tell my story. They listened patiently to every detail. I told the whole story, but when I got to the point when the man actually raped me the details stopped, and I said, "And then he raped me and ran away." They stopped me there and asked me to speak the details, knowing it would be hard for me to open up about that difficult part of the attack. So I did.

In that safe place with soft hands on me, and soft hearts to pray for me, I spoke through my tears and told them everything. Although it was tough, it was so good to get it out. And their healing hands were what I had been craving since the night at the hospital. We closed the night with more prayers and then went our separate ways, bonded by the experience of deep trust, friendship and sisterhood.

In the meantime, things with Trevor became really strained. Our relationship was still very new and we did not have a solid foundation to handle a situation like this. I was an emotional mess and the sheer stress of dealing with what was happening was a lot for any couple to handle, much less one that had only known each other for a month or so. And by default, I had moved in with him. I could not return to my little cottage so soon. It held too much emotional charge for me. So all of a sudden, his new girlfriend was living with him in his tiny one-room place, going through one of the hardest experiences one can imagine. Needless to say he was not ready for that. And understandably so, he became more distant with each day. Eventually we had an argument that ended the relationship entirely.

My own home had not changed since the night of the rape. Furniture was turned on its side and the pillows smeared with my excrement were strewn all over the apartment. The police had picked through everything and had taken many of my belongings as evidence, including my bedding, ripped clothes and the little box that held the money – basically anything the guy had touched. But everything was still a huge mess, infused with fear and a disturbing energy. Yet I didn't want to give the cottage up either. It was my home. The rapist had taken so much from me: my peace of mind, my relationship, my sense of safety, my emotional health and many of my belongings. I did not want him to take my home, too.

My landlord put a new alarm system in the little cottage while I stayed with Trevor during that past week, and motion-sensor flood lights were installed in the back of the house, set to turn on if anyone climbed over the back fence like the rapist had done. And of course I would leave my door locked tight each second I was home. But I still didn't feel safe.

I knew that the man who assaulted me was in jail but I was afraid that his friends or family would try to hurt me out of anger because I went to the police, so I still lived with fear that someone was around every corner out to get me. A woman from the D.A.'s office said that they had never heard of this happening. If he was in some sort of gang, then there might be some concern, but he was not a gang member. It turned out that he was a twenty-eight-year-old homeless man, a muscular 6'3" man who occasionally did construction work just for food money, but relied on stealing for most of his existence, and his family had kicked him out of the house a while back, so he didn't have anyone in his life who would

191

risk their own arrest to hurt me. She said I had nothing to worry about. But still, my nervous system was always in fight-or-flight and I was scared of every little noise.

My little brother, Travis, flew into town to stay with me for a while and help me get my life back in some sort of order. We cleaned the little house, smudged it with sage, prayed and tried to reclaim it. The first night we were going to sleep there we were both anxious. As we lay in bed, talking and trying to make the best of things, the floodlights suddenly turned on in the back of the house. We both gasped in fear and my heart stopped. We jumped to the window that faced the backyard. And in the middle of the brush was a tiny cat, crouching down in fear as the unforgiving light bore down on him. He was a fuzzy little ball with wide eyes shining from the middle of his fur. My brother and I laughed a nervous laugh. We thought it could have been someone trying to break in. The alarm was set, which calmed my fears a little, but still it was a restless night. That place was steeped in bad memories.

The next morning I woke pretty early. My brother was still asleep so I tiptoed over to the bathroom and took a hot shower. The mirror was steamed up when I got out so I opened the window to help dissipate the condensation. The movement of the window tripped the alarm and I jumped about a foot off the floor as the blaring noise surrounded me and thundered for the entire neighborhood to hear. I ran into the living room and tried to turn it off but I couldn't remember the new code. I looked over to my brother who had just been jostled from a deep sleep into a state of panic. He had the remote to the alarm in his hands and I was punching numbers on the panel on the wall, so between us we eventually got the roaring noise to stop. I laughed a little as I hung my head and covered my face with my hands and started to cry. "I can't do this," I said. I was giving it my best, but I knew at that moment I had to move.

This was one of the lowest points in my life.

I had just been raped and beaten and robbed. My boyfriend had left me, so I had heartache on top of all that. There was a good chance I was HIV positive, as the rapist was a confessed druggie, and I did not know what other kinds of STDs I might have contracted. I had no home. I had no money. I felt completely desolate inside.

A couple of days later I got a call from the District Attorney's office. The man they had arrested apparently had a mental breakdown after his arrest. They could not give me details, but his lawyer could not communicate with him at all, and because he was so out of it they found him "unfit to stand trial." He was sent to a high security mental hospital and was being treated with medication and therapy. The woman explained that it was against the law to put someone on trial if they could not understand what was happening to them. She assured me that he was still imprisoned, and explained that the hospital he was in was a maximum-security facility specifically designed to house prisoners who had lost their grip on reality. For the time being, as far as legal procedures were concerned, we were in a holding pattern until he was better. When the psychiatrists found him "fit to stand trial" then we would meet to discuss the court case, but for now we had to wait. This news did nothing to brighten my mood.

Chapter 17

Resources

Thank God for my little brother.

Travis helped me search for apartments online, and we visited several in the neighborhood the cops suggested I move to. It was a farther drive to college and more expensive, but a much safer part of town. I decided after seeing many that I liked the first one I saw the best, and went back and signed the lease. Trav drove me around from place to place, made jokes in his usual way, helped me eat when I needed to and was a rock of support.

I decided to reduce my school schedule to a more manageable load, and had appointments with a therapist at the school about three times a week. She was a professor there but also a trained therapist, and she was a wonderful resource for me to get things off my chest. School ended up being a great intellectual diversion, too. It forced me to concentrate on things other than my life circumstances, and there was a great peace in knowing that I was still on my path working towards graduation, even if it was slower than the pace other people were able to keep up. However, Trevor was there too and was in many of my classes, and seeing him intensified my pain and loss, so I continued to be a mess.

Although the chiropractor I saw the day after the rape urged me to have patience, I also knew that I wanted to embrace my healing journey fully, and I wanted to find some tools to help me do this. I went online and started doing research to see what kinds of therapy were effective for people who experienced trauma like I had. The documents I found stated that acupuncture, EMDR therapy and exercise were the best modalities to heal experiences like this. I was in. At that point, I didn't even have that much strength left in me, but I drew on every molecule of courage I had (sometimes I think I was running on nothing but fumes and prayers) and put one foot in front of the other.

I immediately scheduled an acupuncture appointment. It was the easiest thing to find. I didn't even know what EMDR was and so I put a call out to a therapist friend to help me find someone who offered that therapy, and I was too depressed to exercise at that point.

The acupuncturist welcomed me to her office and asked why I had come. I began to tell the story of what had happened to me recently. She saw in my medical history that I had survived Cerebral Cysticercosis as well. She asked all about that, too. And like most practitioners, she sat wide-eyed as my story unfolded. Then she proceeded to take my pulse in that mysterious Chinese Medicine sort of way. She looked at me and said that my pulse was like someone's who had just come back from a war. I actually felt that way, too. She gave me a treatment to help bring my system back into balance, and I noticed the effects immediately. I wasn't so nervous. My whole body felt more relaxed and less jumpy. It was just a little improvement, but it was a definite improvement, and I saw her for a few months. Each time I got a treatment I felt better. But after a while I was broke. These treatments were expensive.

In California there is an organization that will cover the medical bills for victims of violent crimes. They did cover a certain number of acupuncture treatments, but I only got reimbursed many weeks, sometimes months later, and sometimes not at all. It was a blessing to have even that much assistance, but I eventually ran out of money. However, the acupuncture helped me get in touch with the strength deep inside me so I could carry on and seek out the other help I needed.

I felt that I needed to secure a regular therapist that could see me throughout my entire healing journey. The one from school was a wonderful woman and she was seeing me pro bono, as emergency care the college provided for students, but it was not meant to be long term. I found a woman online and started going to her office. She was sweet. Her name was Betty, and every time I saw her I could see tears well up in her eyes, she had so much compassion for me. Yet I felt that I couldn't let some of my deepest thoughts out, or anger, or some of my deepest pain. I was actually afraid of hurting her. And she did little else other than listen to me for an hour. I didn't feel that it was helping. Betty was nice, but she was not the right therapist for me.

By then my therapist friend had gotten back to me with a referral for someone who practiced EMDR. When I made it to her office I knew right away that she was the right practitioner for me. She not only practiced EMDR but a myriad of other therapy modalities as well. Upon our first meeting, she taught me EFT, and I was excited to have someone on board who had many tools to help me with. That was exactly what I had been looking for.

EFT stands for Emotional Freedom Technique, and is a method that has profound effects for some people. It works by tapping on certain acupuncture meridian points while focusing on traumatic thoughts, memories or feelings. It is simple, and she taught me how to do it in one session. We did it together before I left, and it was quite remarkable how much I calmed down when I practiced it. In our sessions, we would pinpoint a memory that was particularly charged for me emotionally. She then asked me to rank it on a scale of 0 10, with zero being no charge at all, and ten being the most charged I could ever be. Then we would begin tapping on certain points over and over while I talked about what I was charged about. At the end of a round of tapping on places like my forehead, clavicle and fingers, I would then tap the top of my head while saying, "I deeply and completely love and accept myself." I would then say "peace," while I brought the palm of my hand in front of my face down to my lap. It seemed simple – a little too simple to actually do anything. But I swear it worked. After a round of tapping like that, the charge would be brought down a few notches on that scale of 0-10. Then we kept doing more rounds until the charge was next to nothing. It was a relief. I loved it so much I ended up teaching some other friends, and it worked really well for them, too. However, it seemed to work in the moment but not long-term. Perhaps I didn't do it enough, but soon afterwards we began EMDR, and that rocked my world so much that I stopped looking for other tools.

All these acronyms were confusing, but each of them turned out to be amazing therapeutic modalities for me, especially the EMDR. EMDR stands for Eye Movement Desensitization and Reprocessing, and is a modality found to be very effective for people who have experienced trauma of any magnitude. I think it is a mystery as to why EMDR actually works, but the leading theory has been explained to me this way, and it makes sense to me. When you have experiences, they are stored in your brain as memories on the left side of the brain. The left side of the brain is the logical side of the brain, and everything has its proper place. The mind knows what happened today versus yesterday versus last year because of this organization. However, when you experience something that is extremely traumatic and is more than the mind can assimilate, it stores it in the right side of the brain. The right side of our brain is the spacious side. It is the side that is often accessed in times of creativity and meditation, when all things feel connected and time has no meaning. Therefore, the body develops a neural pathway to this memory that it keeps going back to again and again, and the nervous system reacts to it as if it is in the present moment, because the mind does not know that it happened in the past. It is stored in the portion of the brain that is in no-time. Hence, symptoms of PTSD: flashbacks, nightmares, anxiety, fear, fatigue and other symptoms occur. In a way, it is the mind's method to make sure that whatever traumatic thing happened in that moment never happens again, so it keeps you on guard all day, every day, ready to run at any moment. It is wise, in a way, but for a person to have their nervous system in constant fight-or-flight mode is exhausting, and it affects everything in one's life.

When the modality was developed, they were trying to stimulate the brain bilaterally by having the recipient move their eyes back and forth, following the moving finger of the therapist. But after a while, they found that the therapist's arm was getting tired and the recipient's eyes would fatigue before the session was done. Later, they found that a machine with vibrating pads and sounds stimulated the brain bilaterally just as well, and was easier on everyone. When the left and the right sides are activated and open, the therapist reads aloud the description of the patient's triggering memory, and the brain plucks it from the right side of the brain, de-triggers it in a unique way each time, and places it in the left side of the brain, where memories belong. This way, the brain knows it happened in the past, and the body no longer reacts to it as if it is happening in the present moment, thereby relaxing the entire sympathetic response. Then, the therapist calls out resources that the recipient has created during previous sessions. These resources are something personal that gives the recipient strength when thought about. The recipient is given time to imaginatively play out a scene with their resources while the brain is being stimulated bilaterally. Theoretically, these resources are put into the "place" in the right side of the brain where that traumatic memory was. So after a treatment the neural pathway that led to the scary memory now leads straight to the resource, something that will make the person feel stronger.

I worked with my new therapist for quite a while just to get the whole story of the attack and rape out, and to solidify the trust in our relationship. Then she helped me develop my resources, archetypal characters in my imagination that represented beneficial qualities that I could think of and gain benefit from. I had three that I came back to over and over. One was a snow leopard. That animal had shown up in my life over and over and it was already on my mind before the attack. But afterwards, she grew in my imagination until she was a huge cat towering above me. She communicated to me by her actions that I was her cub, and she represented fierce, protective mama energy. She walked around me in clockwise circles with her big, sensitive ears perked up. She was always on guard, with me in the center of her circle. Sometimes I would imagine the rapist coming towards me, and she would go to him in a flash and rip him to shreds with her sharp teeth. She was fast and wild, and while she was on guard, I had nothing to worry about. When she was pacing around me, I could rest. Finally rest. I didn't have to listen for every little sound. I could rest easy, and even go to sleep in peace, and know she had my back.

Another resource was called "Nurture Woman." She was also larger than life and was another mama figure for me. She was so big she was able to hold my adult body like a baby, and she stroked my hair and gave me pure water to drink that seemed to quench my thirst in a way that nothing else ever has. Even her hair, which was long and draped over her shoulders, turned into waterfalls somehow. She had vines growing around her and she had an element of being a natural hot spring or a rain forest. When I was in her arms, I was taken care of, nurtured and loved. And I was again at peace.

The last resource I developed was a vision of me holding my kittens. These two kittens were real, and were at home while I was in therapy. Those two little guys were such good medicine for me. I got them right after the assault when I moved into my new apartment, and their adorable mannerisms, cuddles and love were so good for my soul. During the times I was antisocial and unable to even leave my house, they were there, loving me, interacting with me without judging me; always knowing when I needed a little extra kiss on the nose. In my therapy sessions I would imagine that I was holding them, like Nurture Woman was holding me. I was their mama, like the snow leopard was for me. And it filled me with so much love there was no room left in my heart for anything else.

After developing these powerful resources, we worked on finding the most potent memories of the attack, the snapshots that triggered my emotions the most. The first one I decided to work with was when he burst through the door. That moment when I realized that he wasn't my boyfriend or anyone I knew, and that some bad man was really breaking into my house. It was that moment when my nervous system flew into fight or flight, and it was a moment I kept replaying in my mind all day long, even at school. My therapist wrote down, word for word, my description of that snapshot. Then we got out the EMDR machine. This machine has two vibrating pads that were placed in my palms, as well as headphones, which I put into my ears. The headphones and vibrating pads were synched up, so when the right earpiece made a noise, the right pad in my hand vibrated, and then both the left earpiece and pad would simultaneously turn on. Right, left. Right, left.

Once the machine was on, and we adjusted the volume and intensity to be just right for me, my therapist read out loud, word for word, the memory we decided to work with, the moment the guy broke into my house and I realized he was a "bad guy." I could see the memory before me like a movie, just like I did so many times throughout each day. But this time, my imagination actually changed the outcome of the memory. He came into the door the same way, but as he ran towards me, he got smaller and smaller, and by the time he reached my bed, he was about two inches tall. I reached down and picked him up, and brought him up to eye level. I watched him squirm, trying to get out of my grasp, but my fingers were absolutely huge compared to his body. I looked at him, front and back, reached over and opened my window, and simply threw him outside like he was a bug, then closed my window. Then the movie disappeared before my eyes. When my mind was finished with that scene, my therapist then read to me the descriptions of my resources, one by one. First, I called in the snow leopard. She came and walked around me in a circle, listening intently for any threats. I saw myself in the middle of her circular path, fully relaxed and eventually I fell asleep in my mind's eye, peaceful under her watchful gaze. Then Nurture Woman was brought in. In my minds eye she held me, and her gentle and eternal love was like a salve on my broken heart. We only had to spend a moment with my kittens as a resource, as they spent a lot of real time in my arms and my mind knew that resource well.

Interestingly, each time we did this process for the memories that provoked fear or pain, my brain would do different things to the memories to make them less triggering. The next memory we worked with was the moment when he tore my t-shirt off and I knew he was going to rape me. When she read that back to me, word for word as I had described it to her, I remembered it as it was, but then the memory in my mind began to turn into an old photograph. Then all the colors in the photo morphed into tiny, beautiful ribbons that flowed in the wind, and eventually the small pieces of fabric came away from the picture all together and scattered in the stirring breeze, leaving no picture to see at all. The colorful ribbons were beautiful to watch floating away. And again, she asked me to invoke my resources, and these imaginary beings would come and give me their medicine.

Another time we worked with a memory of him attacking me. In my mind's eye he shrank until he was a boy, and all of a sudden I looked down on myself and I became an old African American woman, his grandmother. I felt him as a little boy, with all his fear and pain, wanting to be loved and held. I felt his childlike heart, and had so much love and compassion for him, that I took him into my arms and just held him, wept with him and nurtured him for a long time.

The memories that my mind was changing were not changed for good. I could still remember the details of the real experience just as clearly as before the EMDR session. It's not like this erased them or even changed them in my mind, but the process simply removed the emotional trigger and intense emotional charge that was attached to the memory. I could then think about it or talk about it, and instead of it bringing up fear, pain or panic that previously felt like a 9 or 10 out of 10, it was brought down to a 1 or 2.

For days after these sessions I felt more open, less depressed, less scared and definitely stronger. I felt like I was walking around in a bit of a daze with my heart more open and my whole system felt more sensitive. The sessions were so powerful that I didn't need to do them often, but when we did one, it shifted things more dramatically than anything else by far.

Chapter 18

And So It Is

About six months after the attack, I felt like I wanted to take a self-defense course to empower me in case another attack happened. I got online and started researching courses in the area. Several of my friends recommended a place that was a dojo for women only. I saw on their site that they had a self-defense class there, but they also sent their teachers into the community to teach off-site if there were enough people to warrant it. The rapist was arrested less than a mile away from my college, so the idea of having the teachers come down to the school to instruct seemed fitting. There are many young women living in that area who attended the college and I was concerned for all of them. The self-defense center said that I needed forty women to sign up in order for them to come teach us, and so I began enrolling women from the school in the course until we had enough. The teachers came down once a week for six weeks, and afterwards I wrote an article about it for our school newspaper:

Dear good readers, this article might contain some material that is difficult to read on an emotional level, so if now is not the right time to read it, I invite you to turn the page and come back to it later, or not. But if you are ready, please read on for a truthful, inspiring journey of healing and self-empowerment for many.

First – the good stuff. Our college recently hosted a self-defense class for women. Three amazing instructors from Hand to Hand Self-Defense Center in Oakland came down to teach the course to nearly forty women on our campus. We learned all sorts of self-defense strategies, including how to use our voice, hands, feet and elbows (and everything else) to help us to get out of potentially dangerous situations. It was pretty fun and amazing, but there was something else that happened in that room that none of us quite expected... And quite frankly, it really blew me away.

(And now onto some harder-to-read stuff.)

The reason I was inspired to bring this self-defense course to our campus was because of a traumatic experience that I endured last April. We were three weeks into our quarter and one night just before bed, a man broke into my house and brutally assaulted me, both physically and sexually. He robbed my house, and ran away into the darkness after nearly killing me while threatening to do so over and over. I spent the night in the hospital and police station, and somehow, miraculously, returned to school the following week. I managed to stay in my classes, with the help of some amazing friends and counselors (you know who you are... thank you from the bottom of my heart). School became the only steady thread in my life and was actually an anchor during a time when my life fell apart at the seams, on every level. Time has passed, and I have done some incredible healing work with chiropractic, therapy and self-healing practices. I finally feel like I am emerging out of a cocoon. And, oh my goodness, it feels good to be able to breathe deeply and know I am healthy and alive!

At one point during my healing process I knew I wanted to take a self-defense course to empower me physically so I could defend myself in the future – just in case. I had always thought it was a good idea to take a self-defense course, but you know, school is busy and lots of good ideas come and go and I never find the time to actually do the things I think about, but at this point it became a priority. Many women in my life recommended the same place, Hand to Hand Self-Defense Center in Oakland. On their website I read that they sent their teachers out on occasion to teach at businesses and schools in the community if there was a large enough group. As soon as I saw that, I knew that I wanted to bring those teachers to our campus. I, with all my heart, did not want anything like what happened to me to happen to any friend, sister, or fellow student in my community. And so the process began. Our student council offered to donate to the project to offset the cost for the participants, the room was reserved, the teachers secured and forty women signed up.

Then the magic occurred. I was absolutely stunned when I saw the power and strength coming out of some of my fellow students and staff during the class. Something special happened when so many women from our college got together in one room. I don't even know if I can explain what it was, but it was palpable. We created a bond in there that I wasn't expecting. And women became empowered in ways that I wasn't expecting either – nor did they expect this. I will let some of the participants share their experience:

"For the first time in my life, I feel like I can take care of myself. I have always relied on traveling in packs and have been scared to be alone. But I really feel like I could defend myself if I needed now. And I have a new level of alertness. I know that sounds funny, but I just mean that I notice what is around me more. And I feel more comfortable yelling. They taught us punches and kicks we could actually do, and really helped tailor what we did to our body type or skill level. I was amazed. The things they taught us were easy and do-able. But in the right combinations we are powerful.

It was also really nice to take this class with so many empowering ladies from the school. What a strength we possess! And it was amazing to see our comfort levels with each other grow in such a short time. When we come together for good, we are unstoppable! I cannot put into words how changed and empowered I feel. Those four hours really changed my life. I feel like I can conquer the world. I do think that class was a self-esteem boost and it reminded me that I am worth defending. So thank you from the core of my being for putting that together. I really do think it changed my life."

~ Audrey M

"I've learned so much through this course: how to search deep within myself for the power that has been long forgotten, physically and mentally. I'm 5'2" and weigh 103 lbs. Prior to the course, I felt weak compared to big, tall guys, so what would happen if one of them were to attack me, the tiny person? It was tough, just to think I would not be able to protect myself! The course has taught me a lot about self-defense for women, regardless of size. I've also learned the power of my voice; of our sisters' voices... they were powerful. The cheers, the talks, the warm-up exercises, the completion ceremony... all of that was so touching and I almost started to cry at the end. But I've learned to be a stronger woman, physically and mentally."

~ Miranda N

"This powerful experience has made me a stronger and more confident woman. I learned physical and emotional ways to protect my well-being that will last a lifetime. I encourage everyone to participate in a self-defense class!"

~ Lauren B

I would like to express my gratitude to the incredible teachers from Hand to Hand, my sisters here at the college who shared that class with me, and everyone who has witnessed me go through one of the hardest experiences of my life, and helped me transform it into a source of service and strength. And so it is.

~ Ashanna Keli

One thing I did not write about in the article was an experience that rocked my world. One day the self-defense teachers led us through an exercise in which we all took turns going to the front of the room. While one teacher got on top of us, holding our arms down to the ground, we had to practice getting out from underneath them using the self-defense technique we had just learned.

It brought up a lot of emotion for me, as being held down by someone on top of me closely mocked the rape. And as I looked around, I saw a few other women in tears, women who had experienced a similar situation. I almost left the room and didn't participate in this exercise because I was so triggered, but I knew it was a safe environment and something inside of me was telling me to do it, even if it was really uncomfortable. I started crying while I was in line, fretting while I watched the women getting pinned down one by one. I did not want to go. But my turn came up, and I went to the front and lay on the floor.

The teacher got on top of me and pinned my arms to the ground. During the rape I was being choked, not pinned down by my arms, but it was close enough and my body was releasing waves of fear, sadness, vulnerability and grief. I had tears streaming from the corners of my eyes and the teacher checked in with me to make sure I was OK and let me know I was safe. She held me down, and I gathered my strength and practiced the moves to get out of it. I was able to reprogram my body to feel safe in a position that it had previously felt threatened in. Surrounded by women friends from the school in this safe, supportive environment, I was able to unwind some traumatic memory. I think I cried for the rest of the evening, but it shifted me, deeply.

I went to the bathroom after the session ended and one of the women in the class approached me. She was a quiet woman, soft and sweet. She had a very wholesome, innocent look to her and she always seemed so gentle and kind. She told me with tears in her eyes that she had been raped years before. She confessed that she had passed out one night at a party (from either alcohol or being drugged, I did not ask) and woke pinned down to the ground by a young man who then raped her. She had never been pinned since then, and that exercise brought up a lot of emotion for her too, but she shared that it was also transformative. She said that it felt more healing than the years of therapy that she went through.

During the next school quarter, the self-defense teachers came back. One night before the class started, I approached one of them and asked her how to specifically get out of the situation of being choked. We had done the exercise of how to get out from being pinned but I wanted to be equipped to get out of the same situation I had been in, because the night I was raped, I tried to get out of his grip on my neck and I could not. I am a strong woman, but nothing I tried was successful. The teacher said there were a few things she could show me and asked me to get on the ground. She proceeded to get on top of me and put her hand right on my throat, just like the rapist did. She then showed me some moves to get out of it, which I never would have thought of. It was brilliant.

I thought that having her hand on my throat would have brought up much more emotion for me, but most of the emotion stored in my body was released when I was pinned to the floor during the quarter before, and there was not that much left any more. So her mock hold on my throat brought up a few tears, but not as much as I would have thought. Now I know how to get out of that situation, too. That course healed and empowered me, and all the women in the class in ways I never expected nor could have experienced otherwise.

Chapter 19

⤫

Healing Circle

About this time, I joined a support group for women who had survived sexual assault. I was hesitant to join the group because I was already so sad at times that I thought listening to so many stories from other women about their experiences of rape and molestation would make me even more depressed. But I needed a community of women who could understand me, and I wanted to join others to walk the path of healing together. It felt like a very lonely road on my own.

The day came for the first meeting. When I arrived, I immediately noticed a huge difference between me and the other women. Every single woman that walked through that door felt like a ghost to me. After we introduced ourselves, we all told our stories of the abuse we had experienced, and how we were doing since the assaults. Most of the women experienced an assault many years ago, some as much as fifteen or twenty years before. And it wasn't their stories that saddened me, it was their health: their sexual, physical, and social well-being. They were each a shell of a woman, barely able to get by in the world. Most of them had not spent much time and energy directed towards their healing and had suppressed it, which led them to withdraw from the world, their bodies and their loved ones. Most were socially awkward, unable to be in relationships, some of them unable to keep a regular job. I cried that night with grief and anger that so much crap happens in the world and that it affects people this way.

My sharing in the circle that night was very different. I told them about EFT and EMDR, how it worked and how much it had helped me. I encouraged them to take care of themselves, and do things that empowered them. I told them about the self-defense course I participated in and how it had helped everyone that did it. I felt like I was on a different plane than most of them, much more in touch with my emotions, with my body, and although the assault I experienced was much more recent than most of them, and much more violent, I felt that I had healed far more than they had.

I left that circle feeling exhausted. It was hard to see firsthand what it looks like if you don't delve into therapy and do anything and everything that can help you. I saw how much people suffer needlessly. There are so many talented and brilliant therapists making such a difference in the world with tools like EMDR and others. I took on my healing as if my life depended on it, and I saw that night that the life I want to live actually did depend on it, because if I didn't take it on with abandon, I would end up just like these women, a ghost of myself – a mere shadow of what once was.

I have a choice.

And I know what I choose.

I choose my life.

And I choose my joy.

I am reminded of a song that I learned in a ceremony. Once I learned this song, I sang it, and still sing it, all the time. It fills me with strength and a remembrance of my essence, my strength, and why I have to carry on when I feel bruised and beaten to the bone.

A woman who loves herself,
Cannot be broken.
A woman who loves herself,
Will never fall.
A woman who loves herself,
Cannot be broken.

A woman who loves herself,
Will never fall.
And I, I'm singing this song for my healing.
And I, I'm singing this song for my freedom.
And I, I'm singing this song for creation,
And I, I'm singing this song for love.

(Author unknown; words adapted by me.)

Another core part of my healing journey came directly through my body. While I was still in New Zealand, a wonderful thing started up in Oakland called Ecstatic Dance. It is held in a 13,000 square foot ballroom with a sprung wooden dance floor, and DJs with or without live musicians play music for about three hours. There is only one rule: no talking on the dance floor. There is no alcohol sold there, only healthy organic treats and free filtered water. There is no choreography taught, no expected way for you to move your body, only an open invitation for you to feel into your own body deeply and see what arises and to put that into motion. It was like a dream come true for me. Many of my friends had emailed me about it when I still lived in New Zealand and I was wildly jealous that I couldn't go. So the very night I flew back to California, a dear friend picked me up from the San Francisco airport. We went to get a healthy dinner at the Whole Foods Market in Oakland (which completely blew my mind after shopping in the little shops in New Zealand) and went straight to Ecstatic Dance.

I had a blast.

After twenty-something hours of flying and airport stays, I was shaking my body and moving to great music and reconnecting with old friends through hugs and movement. I was exhausted but in love with this opportunity to dance in a clean and uplifting environment. Twenty-two days later, the assault happened.

A few weeks after the attack, I went back to the dance. After just a few minutes I began crying. It literally hurt to be embodied. There was so much emotional and physical pain stored inside of me that just to focus on being in my body was agonizing. But I went anyway because I knew it was good for me and I knew it was a way for me to heal. I kept going for months and kept crying each time. My friends would see me on the dance floor, and give me a look of concern but because there was no talking allowed it gave me a safe space to just do my thing and dance my sadness and leave when I needed to without anyone asking me what it was about. Months went by and I danced. And eventually my dance became less heavy, less painful. I danced my torment and discomfort, danced my prayers for healing and put my emotions into movement.

This environment wasn't about looking good; it was about showing up to sweat out the crap stored in your body that you didn't need any more. It was about shaking out your tight spots and finding the places in your body that still stored tension, and stretch it and move it and yell it and dance it. It was about expressing your self through authentic and liberated movement, and so much more.

Eventually my dance became lighter. When the music hit the crescendo and everyone was jumping and shaking everything with abandon, eventually I was dancing my joy and breathing deep breaths simply because I could. I was dancing my ecstatic, raw, gratefulness to be alive. It was amazing to see how my dance and my body transformed as I released the tension I stored through my own practice of moving with freedom. It took a long time. Yet it was wonderfully worth it.

Yoga proved to be another great way for me to heal through my body as well. I often didn't have the strength to go running or exercise in any other way but I could go into the peaceful setting of a yoga class and do what someone else told me to do. I often cried at the beginning of my healing journey, as being present in my body so directly was difficult. But the stretching component of the poses released emotions held in my body, while the strengthening action of the poses helped me develop internal strength as well. I felt like the physical practice cleansed me inside and out, slowly, in an honoring way, and helped me move my body towards its optimal alignment to encourage the nervous system to calm down. The focus on breath was essential for my healing too, considering that my breath was cut off during the attack. The pranayama, the extension of the life force, or breath, induced a state of peacefulness in a way that nothing else did.

The philosophy that was woven into the yoga classes helped me too. It helped keep my fire alive to live love and transform my challenges in life to be of service to myself and to the world. It reminded me to trust in the Divine play, in the perfection of the Great Mystery of the way things are, and to know that this rape, those brain tumors, all of this, happened in my life for a reason. I knew that I was meant to serve the world as a healer, and to be honest, just writing this book solidifies that purpose inside me even more.

I have read many narratives of women healing from rape by now. One common thread I have found is that the most profound healing for all these women came from having a voice. When they wrote about what happened to them, or spoke about it, became an activist or volunteered to help others, it was the key to their healing more than anything else. It has been doubly healing for me to write this book and become vocal about the rape, since during the attack I was choked, with my throat closed off. So opening it, expressing myself in these ways, is tremendously freeing and medicinal. I am grateful that I have come to a place where I want to sing and shout out my message of hope! I encourage you to find your own voice and share in whatever ways you feel called to.

At the women's circle that came together right after the rape, one of the ladies told me that my body needed some gentle, loving hands-on healing and suggested I see a massage therapist. She said she knew of the perfect person for that. Another friend said she also had someone in mind that would be great. These two women had never met before that night, and yet later on, when I went to get the names of the therapists they were talking about, they were both thinking of the same person. If I lived in a small town it would make more sense, but I live in the Bay Area with millions of people. So this synchronicity made me feel the magic of what was happening, and that this massage therapist would be a special person for me to see, and she was.

I have never met anyone like this woman. She is ten years younger than me but she holds more loving mother energy than almost anyone I have ever been around. Her massages were amazing, and her voice and use of imagery and breath were incredible. Most of all, she was deliciously feminine, and I felt wrapped up in the Divine Mother while I was in her presence, so nurtured and held. Months after the attack, she invited me to join her at a women's retreat. I didn't even ask for more information before I said yes. That retreat ended up providing a missing piece of my healing journey that I didn't even know I needed.

The retreat was designed to be a rite of passage for women, something that our culture is sorely lacking. It was a wonderful retreat in general, but in the middle we did an exercise that was profoundly healing for me. There were about fifteen participants, and we formed a circle around a red candle. We were asked to speak aloud things that made us angry. The idea was that we would get in touch with our anger, get it out and give it to the fire, as symbolized by the candle.

We all started voicing the things in the world and in our lives that made us angry. "I am angry that women don't have freedom in parts of the world," someone shouted. "I am angry that I have to do all the house-cleaning and my husband never helps me!" another woman exclaimed. "I am angry that my dad is an alcoholic and that he treated our family like crap because of the booze!" We all went on like this for a while, and slowly, music began in the background, gradually increasing in volume.

When we had been yelling and offering things to the fire for a while, we were given time to get our anger out in a more physical way. There were foam cylinders for us to beat the walls with, mattresses for us to lie on, pillows to punch and kick. The music was turned up super loud and we were invited to go punch, scream, to kick and thrash our anger out in any way we wanted. At first I had a really hard time getting into it. I roamed around the room and hit the wall, trying to participate like a "good girl" but it felt extremely forced and very awkward. I hit the walls with the foam rollers with little grunts of forced emotion.

But after fifteen or twenty minutes of watching other women really go for it, something inside me stirred and I began to feel angry. The music was pumping at this point and I ended up lying down on a mattress. All of a sudden the rape started replaying in my mind. I could feel him on top of me, his hands at my throat. I could hear his voice telling me that he was going to kill me. I could feel him move in between my legs and begin to have sex with me completely against my will.

And I got angry.

I got downright full of rage.

And I started kicking.

And I started screaming at him.

I called him every terrible name I could think of and told him to fuck off and go to hell about a million times. I punched at him and kicked at him and cried and cried until I was red in the face and then some.

The facilitator had taken time with each of us at the beginning of the retreat to ask us about our lives, and she knew what I was facing in that moment. She and some other assistants came and watched over me, held my head, wiped my sweat as I cussed and screamed and kicked my attacker. I did this for so long. I don't even know how long I did this. I screamed until I had nothing left. I punched and kicked until I could not move any more. I was covered in sweat and became completely hoarse and exhausted. But I kept going until there was absolutely nothing left inside of me.

Over the previous months I had been told many times, in therapy and by friends, that I needed to get in touch with my anger. I had tried. I tried to talk about it while I was on the couch in the therapist's office, but that is hardly letting anger out, saying in a calm voice, "I am very angry. I have anger." But this exercise gave me a safe space for pure, raw emotion to come out. And come out and come out until there was nothing left. They wouldn't let me stop until I was done. When I stopped because my throat was raw, they gave me water and told me to keep going. When I stopped because I was exhausted, they encouraged me to find strength inside that I didn't know was there to keep going. And I went, until there was nothing left. Not a drop of rage left. Not a single drop.

After the rape happened I gave every thought about the attack full attention when it entered my mind. I wanted so badly to heal fully and I felt that if I repressed the memories, I would be hindering and prolonging the healing process. So when a memory came, I would bring it fully into my awareness, remember the scene, explore my thoughts around it, and feel the emotions as fully as possible. However, there were times when I was constantly barraged with memories from the rape, and sometimes I was not in a place that was conducive to delving into those thoughts, but I would do it anyway. Sometimes I would cry in the middle of class, while driving or in company of friends. I had these things going on inside me that had nothing to do with my external environment or the present moment and they wanted out.

But about a year and a half after the assault I began a spontaneous practice that became a huge landmark in my healing. I went with some dear friends to a music festival and the first day, in the middle of the music and celebration, memories of the rape came up. As usual, I let myself be with them and feel the emotions attached to the thought. But I wanted, at that festival, to be free of it. I had been diligently going to therapy for so long and swimming in the deep waters of emotional healing. This weekend I wanted to be on vacation from all of that.

There was a moment at the festival when I realized that right before a thought or memory of the rape came, there was a little tickle in my brain, the same type of sensation that occurs when I am trying to remember a name or fact, and I can somehow feel in my brain when I am getting close to remembering it. The sensation was slight, but it was there. I was able to isolate that feeling, and catch my memories before they actually came into my mind. I was able to go out into thought-land and talk to the memory before the picture came into my head. I spoke directly to the thought and said to it, "I thank you for coming. And you know that I will honor you. But now is not the time. Please come back later, and I will give you all the air time you need." And it would go away, just like that. The picture would not again enter my mind and I was able to enjoy the present moment without the past interfering with my experience.

I spent the whole weekend practicing this, and for the first time in a year and a half I was able to spend an entire day without thinking about the rape. But several times a day, I had those conversations with the thoughts coming to visit me. It was freeing, and I felt liberated from being a victim. But I did honor those thoughts and memories later. I always came back to them and asked them what they held for me, and felt fully all the emotions they brought. I truly believe that had I not come back to those thoughts, that they would have festered inside of me and been very counterproductive to my healing process.

There were times when I did not know what else to do to heal. I knew that I wanted, with all my heart, to transform this situation with love, into love, and some of the time I felt that I was doing that. But there were also times when I regressed into feeling like such a victim. I couldn't help but be envious of the people around me whose lives seemed so easy compared to my own. I got angry and felt helpless. At one point, I emailed all my friends and asked them for help and guidance. It does not come easy for me to ask for help when I need it, and I felt like I wasn't strong enough to handle it on my own, and that was embarrassing. But there is absolutely no reason for me to handle it all on my own. That is what friends are for, right?

I told them that I was having trouble getting out much but that I missed them. I explained clearly that I was feeling like a victim at times and that I needed their help in healing this trauma. I asked them, "How do you transform your own challenges into love?" because I felt all out of answers. I invited them to come over for a meal and talk about it, or for them to just write me an email and give me insight into their own methods. They all showed up for me. I had friends coming over with bags full of groceries, making me breakfast and offering support and guidance. Some told me that they practiced forgiveness, including forgiving themselves, and asked if I had done this. I felt that I had. Some said that just by setting the intention for the pain to transform into love would help it be so in the end. Some said that in times of need, they talked to their friends about things, just like I was doing, and this helped them even if their friends didn't have all the answers. To be honest, it helped me too. Just offering up my truth, my naked, vulnerable truth to my loved ones was the thing that helped. It helped them all to see me, the whole me, in my weakness as well as during my times of strength. And their support and guidance was wonderful.

Chapter 20

The Voice of Grace

December 10, 2010 ~

I found out just a few days ago that the man who broke into my home almost two years ago and nearly choked me to death, beat me, raped me and robbed me, is finally fit to stand trial. He was examined by the court psychiatrists and was released by the mental institution ready to start the court proceedings. I was told that the entire trial process would take one and a half to three years, on the conservative side, the lawyer said.

The thought of getting up in front of a courtroom and giving my testimony weighs on me. It is in the future but it is looming and continually absorbs a lot of my energy. I wonder if the defense attorney will grill me and try to discredit me like I've seen in the movies. Also, the thought of having to voice what happened in such detail in front of a bunch of unknown people is challenging, to say the least.

It isn't only giving my testimony that seems daunting, though. It is going to be the first time I will see the man that attacked me in broad daylight. I never saw his face that night when he broke into my house. He had his hoodie cinched around his face so I only saw his eyes for a few seconds before he pulled the cord leading to my bedside lamp and everything went into blackness. I have never seen a photograph of him and I still don't know what he looks like.

I imagine being in the courtroom and looking over and seeing him, seeing his face, and even the thought of it sends chills up my spine. It just seems like it would be a lot to take in. And then to have to get up and relive every detail of that assault in front of a lot of people I don't know, right after seeing him for the first time... Ugggghh.

December 15, 2010 ~

I received another call from the District Attorney's office a couple of days ago. His lawyer said that they want to do a deal, and I need to decide how much time I feel comfortable with him serving, as my lawyer cannot make a bargain with the defense attorney if I do not also agree on the amount of time he is to serve. He said that the decision is not up to me ultimately, but that the defendant would probably take the amount of time we offered. He told me that the defendant was being charged with six crimes, and the range of jail time for those six crimes combined is twenty-five to forty years. He said that if we went to trial, he would definitely be found guilty for all six crimes, and that the judge would probably give him life with or maybe even without parole, so they want to make a deal instead. So he needs to know if I want him to serve twenty-five years? Forty? Or life?

What? How do I decide something like this?

I feel like I am inadvertently being given the job of the judge, given power to decide how much time is appropriate to serve for someone who has done something like that. I don't feel like I can prescribe a number of years for the crimes he committed. Who decided those ranges, anyway? It all seems so random in a way. And is he being put away as punishment for what he did that night two years ago? Or is he being put away to keep the public safe in case he would do it again?

I asked some friends for help. One woman said that her mom was a psychic and that she would ask her for some guidance. She came back to school yesterday and told me that her mom said that I needed to put him away for as long as possible because he was going to hunt me down after he got out, and that I needed to move away and hide from him... This did nothing but make me afraid. I had another friend who works for the state as a psychiatrist and I spent a long time on the phone with him last night. I told him that I was leaning towards the twenty-five years instead of more. I could not fathom what twenty-five years would be like in an environment like prison. I asked, "Can he heal? Do you think he will come after me like that woman's mom said? How do I decide something like this?"

I cannot describe how heavy this burden seems to me. The only experience I can draw on is when I got put on "restriction" during high school for several months and that seemed like an eternity. Twenty-five years? *Forty?* The guy isn't even that old. My psychiatrist friend has a good head on his shoulders. Not only does he have lots of experience dealing with the criminals in the court and prison system, but he is also of similar heart and mind to me, and he understands my spiritual and emotional dilemma in this decision. He said he supported me in choosing to believe that this guy could indeed heal, even if it would be a miracle. He told me that prisoners hardly ever seek out the person they assaulted when they are released, and that this woman's mom was probably talking out of her own fear and protective mom side of herself. My own mama told me to give him forty. Actually most moms say that.

But I have to decide. *By tomorrow.* The weight of this man's future is heavy on my shoulders. Do I decide out of fear or out of love and belief in his healing?

Well, when I look at it this way…

I think I know my answer.

January 8, 2011~

Three days ago I got a phone call from the Victim's Advocate from the D.A.'s office. She said that he took the deal of twenty-five years. The attorney from the D.A.'s office was not willing to allow the two years he has already spent locked up in the hospital to be shuffled into the twenty-five years, so in total he will spend twenty-seven years behind bars. He entered a plea of guilty to all six crimes he was charged with, and the final sentencing is scheduled for February 16th.

There was an invisible cord coming right out of my belly that was connected to him and this trial that continually drained the emotional and physical energy out of me during these last two years. When I got that call I felt that cord being cut. I felt a huge weight taken off of me. Now that energy has been re-routed back into myself, and I feel infused with more vitality and joy. I have a vision of my soul skipping down a pathway and jumping up to click happy heels together. Finally.

January 30, 2011 ~

The day of sentencing is approaching. In less than three weeks I will face the man who raped me. In front of the court I will be given the opportunity to speak to him, to share my heart and get anything off my chest that I want to before he is taken to prison. Julie, the Victim's Advocate from the District Attorney's office, had told me over a year ago that I would have this opportunity one day. The court grants all victims of crime the chance to speak to the defendant before they are taken away.

It is a precious opportunity for me. I feel so blessed that I am one of those few women whose perpetrator was caught, and I get to have this kind of closure and peace, knowing that this man will not be lurking behind any corners.

Ever since she told me I would be able to talk to him this way, I have been crafting my message in my heart. But I wasn't expecting it to be this soon. Now the day is coming upon me and I have the challenge of succinctly articulating a vast ocean of emotion, hopes, prayers and truth into a speech that will hopefully wiggle its way into him, something he can hear, understand and hopefully take to heart. There is so much.

There is so much in my life to reflect on, to try and encapsulate in my address to this man. I feel that this is so much bigger than me, than the rape, than him. He is a homeless African American man who, after he broke into my home and violently attacked me and raped me, ranted to me in his own passionate words about how white people were racists and elitists, as if I were personally responsible for the racism in this world and his suffering, and he wanted me to pay for it. Ironically, my mind was completely immersed in the horror of racism, as I was reading a book called Black Elk Speaks when he burst through the door. This book is a detailed account of how white men appeared on the soil of what is now America and invaded the land, slaughtered the Buffalo herds and forced the Sioux nation onto a reservation.

I also need to reflect back to my time in the U.S. Peace Corps over a decade ago, when I was sent to northern Namibia. I was the only white person living in a village of about 10,000 people. Namibia had gained independence from the apartheid South African government just a few short years before I arrived, so the only white people some of the villagers had ever seen before me were white South African soldiers there to enslave them. I heard terrible stories of their huts being run over by tanks, their women raped, their men torn from their families and forced to work in the mines in the south. So when these villagers saw me, a white woman in their remote village, they immediately looked at me with suspicion. However, when I greeted them in their native tongue and they saw that I was there to live with them, learn from them, and serve them, they brightened and welcomed me wholeheartedly. But some of the children who couldn't understand who I was or why I was there would cry immediately upon seeing me, filled with fear.

When I left that village after living there for over two years, I had a going away party, and nearly a hundred people came to honor me. Upon their request, I gave an impromptu speech. What came from my heart was a message of love and gratitude, and it wound its way to be a message of equality as well. I felt that they needed to hear from a white person's mouth that people of all color were equal, that we were all human beings with the same hearts. However, even though I grew up in the United States, a country boasting "equality," I knew that equality hardly exists anywhere. Even the U.S. is full of terribly racist people. I grew up in a small town in Georgia with "Christians" who would go to church and sing the hymns about the love of Jesus and in their next breath condemn the "niggers" for anything and everything. And I know that there is still anger simmering in the hearts of some, and rightly so.

Even in Namibia most of the whites I came across (besides volunteers) were racist towards any non-white person. And the "colored" as they called themselves, people who were a mix of black and white, felt like they were somehow better than the lighter skinned blacks, and those lighter skinned tribes were racist against the darker skinned people. The village where I lived was home to the blackest of them all, and they felt racism from every direction. And they, in turn, treated their animals with total disrespect. They would beat them needlessly, and I assumed it was because it was the only place in life where they felt they had power – and most humans crave power, it seems.

It was clear to me that the man who raped me did what he did to feel power over someone, even if only for a moment. So I know I am not only addressing him in this speech, but his upbringing, his ancestors who suffered so much because of their race, his socioeconomic status, his pain – all of it. It is symbolic of white versus black. Woman versus man.

But here is the kicker – it is also love versus fear.

Compassion and forgiveness versus hatred and the hunger for power.

The rape happened almost two years ago, and I have given myself over fully to the path of healing from this, in every way I have known to try. I want with all my heart to transform this situation into something good, into something that will serve others – an alchemical transformation that turns the poison into love.

This experience has called on every ounce of strength and hope from every cell in my body, continually, for longer than I thought I could possibly hold out. But somehow there was always enough strength to get up another day and keep going. Enough strength to face the sadness, the anger and feel it fully. To cry and cry until there was nothing left. To kick and scream and punch pillows and kick the mattress and allow the rage to have a voice.

I can't even count the number of therapy sessions I have been to, the number of other healing sessions I have had, or the number of times I have talked my dear friends' ears off trying to make sense of this. I have listened to my yoga teachers speak of the path of love and I committed over and over again to walk the path of a yogini, a way of a spiritual discipline where I am engaged fully on the mental, emotional and physical level.

And now I sit, trying to integrate all that I have learned into a message for a man who assaulted me in the most terrifying way imaginable.

February 4, 2011 ~

I was told the day after he was arrested, almost two years ago, that he wrote me an apology letter. The police said they couldn't give it to me because it was an official piece of evidence. But a few days ago I got a call from the D.A.'s office and the letter was read aloud to me over the phone. As best as I can remember, it said something like this:

> I don't expect you to forgive me but I am sorry for what I did. My heart is in the right place but sometimes I do things that are out of my control. Don't make the same mistake I did because I have never had a chance in this life.

I assume that what he meant in the last sentence was the continuation of the cycle of pain in the world. I can only imagine how much he has suffered in his life, from the time he was a small child up to now. And he, as a grown man, has hurt others as a result. I understand that he was never given the tools to help him heal, to help him get to the point where he felt he could choose otherwise. I feel blessed for the teachers I have had in my life, to have been loved so much by my family and friends, to have had the opportunity to heal using the best therapy modalities available.

But I believe, in my heart of hearts, that this man can still come to realize that his essence is still inside him, untouched by all the pain. That essence of true love, the very definition of love itself. I want with all my heart for him to find that inner strength of love, to experience it, to know it in the core of his being, and to live it.

Can he find that in prison? Can he find that in an environment that would probably drain the life and joy out of me in a heartbeat?

Yes. I do believe it is possible. Somehow. And I need to let him know that. I need to look him in the eye and let him know of my own vulnerability and humanity, let him know that I see his vulnerability and humanity, and that my innermost essence honors his innermost essence. I need to speak to his heart in a way that communicates how much pain I have been through as a result of what he did to me, how I have been shaken to the core, but that I forgive him. Truly.

I wish for him to find his true essence, no matter how much pain he has been through in this life, or how much pain he has caused. There is still a human spirit in him that is beyond all of that pain, and that is what I choose to see in him, and what I want him to see in himself.

The question is how do I say this? Will he be able to hear me, understand me?

This is an opportunity to speak a message of love to him that he might never get from another person on this earth. So I have taken up this challenge of crafting this message in such a way that it hopefully works its way into his heart to help carry him through the most terrible times in the most terrible place I can think of ever being on earth. And I must be able to speak these sentences, the most important sentences of my life so far, while looking upon his face for the first time, while I am raw, vulnerable, scared, shaken up and filled with emotion.

February 9, 2011 ~

The time has come for me to write my message to the man who raped me. The court date is now only one week away, and the challenge of articulating all that is in my heart into a concise message has been a challenge. I have sincerely asked for help and guidance from friends, teachers and Spirit. And the time is now. I must begin.

Hello. My name is Ashanna Sevin. I am a human being. What you did to me that night has affected my life in every single way. I have been through so much darkness, so much pain, so much fear, so much anger, rage… and tears, so many tears. Sometimes I wonder if they are ever going to stop. But I have found an essence inside of me, an essence of pure love. I have had to return to that place in me over and over again to heal, to find strength and resilience that I did not know existed.

Who I am – who I choose to be, is someone who lives love.

Someone who transforms everything into love – including this.

So I stand before you now, raw, vulnerable and in my truth when I say, with total honesty, that I forgive you.

I completely and totally forgive you.

You, Reggie Leonard Jones, are a human being. And I know you have gone through so much pain in this life I cannot even imagine.

But I believe that you, too, have an essence inside of you that is pure love. That beyond any pain you have been through, or caused in this life, that essence remains pure and untouched.

And I will pray for you, in all the ways that I pray, that you find that place in you. And when you are in that place in you, and I am in that place in me, we are the same. We are one.

Sometimes I have visions.

Sometimes they come true and sometimes they don't.

I had a powerful vision about you.

You were helping little kids and teenaged boys – kids who grew up in the same kind of neighborhood you did, facing the same challenges in our culture that you have.

And you were helping them.

Helping them choose love, and choose forgiveness.

Because that is what this world needs.

And it was a beautiful vision.

Will it come true?

I don't know.

You choose.

You have to choose it.

You choose.

I spoke my message to Reggie Jones. I looked right into his eyes and conveyed those words with all my heart.

He never looked away. He looked right at me and soaked it all up.

My body was shaking. The Victim's Advocate, Julie, had her hand on my back and she helped me stay steady both emotionally and physically.

I went out into the hall after the trial was declared complete and several strangers came up to me. One younger gentleman said, "Thank you so much for that. That is a lesson in love and forgiveness that I will carry with me forever."

Another woman came up to me and said, "I was raped a long time ago, and I never reached that point of forgiveness. That is truly inspiring, and I will take this to heart and do some work to forgive him like this."

That is when I started to see how this message was for others too, as well as for him and myself.

My friends then escorted me to the District Attorney's office. I met privately with Julie, the Victim's Advocate, and John, one of the detectives that worked on my case. John proceeded to tell me things about the case and Reggie Jones that I did not know.

He explained that just a week and a half before Reggie broke into my home he had stabbed his aunt in the abdomen many times. She did not die, but was hospitalized and was in critical condition, so he was already a wanted man. They had been looking for him, and he had been roaming the streets with nowhere to go during those ten days in total fear, avoiding the police. It wasn't until he was arrested that they knew it was the same man who committed both crimes.

Also, when they processed his DNA a few weeks after he was arrested, an exact match came up for a very similar, unsolved rape case from his small hometown that happened several years before. The woman was at home alone, and was seen through her bedroom window. A masked man broke into her home, and she was choked, beaten and raped, just like me. They had no suspects until Reggie's DNA came up as an exact match.

However, John said that for some reason the small town police force was not taking action to open the case again. He said he would try his best to convince them to reopen the file and try him for this rape as well.

Then I was given access to Mr. Jones's file.

It had all sorts of information in it. I am assuming that some of it was from the police and their interrogation and some of it was from when he was in the hospital. I was able to read his confession about the night of the rape and all about his upbringing. It was a very sad story.

His mother was very ill the whole time he was growing up and his experience of her was that even as a small child, he needed to take care of her instead of her taking care of him.

Also, his cousin sexually abused him for years.

And then there was his father, who was a serial rapist and murderer. I do not know how many women he attacked, but he was arrested for raping multiple women, slitting their throats afterwards, killing them.

After his father was imprisoned, he killed a few more people in prison and is on death row right now.

I began to imagine a young boy, impressionable and openhearted, learning how to be in this big world, but having these terrible experiences, influences and teachers around him.

229

No wonder he turned out this way, I thought.

I would have too if I had been surrounded by all of that.

It deepened my compassion for him even further – until that was all that was left.

I left the courthouse and went to my favorite little teahouse with my friends who had come to support me that day. We celebrated the closure of such a huge chapter in my life. I was still in a bit of shock after reading through Mr. Jones's file and was trying to integrate all that had happened. But my friends filled me with love and helped me feel grounded again. We didn't have that much time at the teahouse, as I had to leave to catch a flight I had booked weeks before they had set the court date. I was lucky that the court time was 8:00 a.m. and my flight left at 2:00 p.m.

I boarded the plane, swimming through the thoughts of the day and flew to Colorado to see my family. My little brother Travis and his wife had twins just a few weeks before. So that night I ended this epic day with two wonderful little babies in my arms. The beginning of a beautiful new chapter.

After a week of good family time with my brother, his wife and boys, my mama and sweet stepfather, I flew to Costa Rica to join my friends for a yoga retreat. We spent nine days filled with beach time, laughter, yoga, meditation, swimming, surfing, soaking up the sunshine and dancing. My definition of heaven! My birthday was during the retreat, one reason I splurged on this whole trip, and on that day the teachers also celebrated me during the classes so I received an abundance of love all day long.

That afternoon, after an amazing yoga asana class, one of the students got up to offer a song to the class; she had such a sweet, angelic voice. My body was tired from a strong practice and I felt open and spent. I was lying on my back in a gorgeous room overlooking a pristine beach. I had just seen my family the week before and had experienced so much birthday love the whole day from good friends as well as strangers, and there, listening to this woman's clear voice, I began to cry.

I was feeling so much bliss.

And then, I had a moment of deep realization.

The moment I had prayed for during my healing process had finally arrived. When I was in therapy after the rape I prayed that one day I would experience joy and bliss to the same degree as all the darkness, sadness and grief that I had endured during my life, especially during that period after the assault. And something inside me, there in Costa Rica in that yoga class said, "This is it. This is that moment. Wake up. It's finally here!"

What was so wonderful was that it was a sustainable state of being. It didn't just last that day. It was day after day after day, week after week, even after I returned back to a very demanding schedule at the chiropractic college. I didn't expect to experience such a tremendous shift after the trial, but I did, and I am ever grateful.

Chapter 21

Sexual Healing

Sex.

Sex after the rape was a tremendous challenge.

After the assault I read many accounts of women healing from rape. I wanted to see how others handled it and see if I would or could have a normal sex life again. But one thing I constantly found in these women's stories, even if they had eventually found happiness and now had full lives, was that their sex life was either nonexistent or not healthy and enjoyable. Many of the women were not able to be in an intimate relationship again, even twenty years after the incident.

It saddened me at first; then I became filled with anger towards my attacker, not just for what he did that night but for the effects it might have on me for a lifetime. I was overcome with hopelessness when I read account after account about women who could not engage in healthy sexual relationships any more.

But my sexuality did blossom and heal over time as a result of all the other healing work I did, along with some amazing experiences I had with two very special men.

My sex drive totally disappeared for many months after the rape. I went deep into a cocoon for a long time, not turned on by anyone or anything. During the first year after the rape, I had sex a few times with a dear friend of mine. He did not have a girlfriend, and although we did not want to be in a romantic relationship with each other, every now and then we succumbed to our base desires. And each time I was flooded with memories of the rape. Sometimes I cried. Sometimes I had no tears but I was in agony, despite the superficial pleasure my body was feeling. It was torturous. Yet my body was confused because the high sex drive I had before the rape was still tugging at my sleeves. But each time I tried it was so emotionally challenging it was hardly enjoyable.

I was terrified that this would not change. But it did.

Over a year after the assault, I met a man who sparked something in me. He was a tall, sensitive, fluid and beautiful dancer with a huge glowing smile. I watched him dance and interact with people, and I felt something stir in me that I had not felt in a long time. It was a gift just to feel turned on again, and I was ready to allow it to be just that.

However, after a few long dates of talking and sharing our life stories, he asked me to be his lover. I felt flooded with joy, yet at the same time I was hesitant. I had all sorts of stories wrapped up around why someone would not want to date me at that point. I felt like I was "damaged goods," with baggage that people would not want to deal with. But Jordan was a healer by nature and was interested in working with me to help heal the trauma through our lovemaking.

The first night that we were physically intimate we were lying on the floor of my living room. We were stretching and massaging each other and he started kneading my legs. He touched a place on my left inner thigh and all of a sudden I started crying.

That place had not been touched since I was raped.

Jordan was touching the exact place where the rapist had forced my leg open in order to penetrate me.

The tears began to flow and he asked what was held in that part of my leg, as he caressed it gently. I told him about the rapist holding my leg there, and after he listened earnestly to my words, he began to talk to my leg, thanking it for holding so much since the attack, while lovingly massaging it. He was talking to that part of my leg as if it were a child,

234

acknowledging how good it was for working so hard, holding such pain for me for so long, and he told my leg it was now alright to let it go.

I allowed my tears to flow and allowed the tension to leave my thigh.

This date happened after I had already developed the practice of asking surfacing memories to come back at a later time if the moment was inappropriate to deal with them, so later, as we started to make love, I was able to practice this technique and be with him without thoughts or memories of the rape entering my mind. I was so grateful for that.

As we made love the second time, he gently went to that place on my left inner thigh. He was right in between my legs, just like the rapist, but he was gentle, loving the parts of me that were previously used and disrespected. He continued to talk to my leg, honoring it, and I felt the tension that was previously held there melt away. I cried, as much for the pain that was releasing as for the gratitude that welled up in my heart for such a gentle, loving man to be serving me in this beautiful way.

Six months later I met the love of my life. His name is José, and he is my beloved, my life partner and my healer. I started falling for him before I even met him. I saw him on the dance floor at Ecstatic Dance, and for months I knew him only through his self-expression and movement, and I was attracted to him right away. Finally, we began to speak, and weeks later he confessed he had a crush on me. I was delighted to tell him that it was mutual and we set up our first date.

He is a passionate lover, and upon walking through my door that night, he took me into his arms right away and began kissing me with deep longing. We tumbled onto the floor locked in a yummy embrace and he pinned my arms to the ground while devouring my neck with kisses and love bites. But after a while I started to panic.

I had been pinned down like that by the woman from the self-defense course and had done some healing around that situation, but having a man on top of me in an atmosphere charged with sexual desire triggered my memories of the assault in a powerful way. Although I was totally attracted to him, I started to cry and become short of breath. I had to ask him to stop and we proceeded to talk about why. He listened with the most gentle, loving heart, and offered himself to act as an instrument of my healing, if he could.

José is a talented artist and graphic designer, not a healer by profession, but I discovered that he is gifted in that realm, too. About two months into our relationship, we were making love, and he began to place his hand on my throat in a conscious attempt to help heal that area. He checked in with me repeatedly, making sure that I knew that I was safe and loved. And as he choked me gently, then harder, I allowed the tears to stream down my cheeks. I reached up and grabbed his wrists, just like I did with the rapist, but instead of trying to pry his hands off of me with all my might, I began to press his hand harder and harder onto my throat. The difference being that I was in control of the pressure. That was the tipping point, the moment when my throat felt safe and honored. Finally the trauma and tension held in my throat faded away, and I felt my body hunger for more, for him to enter into my whole system even farther and deeper, through my throat, through my sex, and through my heart.

Weeks later we purposefully reenacted the rape with gentleness and consciousness. He held my leg open with his hand on my left upper thigh, with his other hand on my throat while he penetrated me, checking in with me, and telling me over and over that he loved me, that I was completely safe, and that we could stop at any moment if I just said the word. I never did have to use the word to stop it, though. It was intensely healing. By placing myself in that position in a loving way, I felt the remaining emotions held in my body leave me, and my system no longer carries the trauma like it did. This type of healing would have never have occurred by talking to my therapist. It could not have happened with a massage therapist. This depth of healing needed to occur within intimate connection with my partner, and I am ever grateful that he had the intuition and courage to love me in that beautiful, healing way.

My relationship with José continues to grow in sweetness and pure love. He has been a rock for me, and with me, while I continue to heal from the mistrust that had grown in my heart as a result of the assault. The fact that I had placed my trust in humanity and left my door unlocked many moons ago, and had my sacred space invaded and plundered, left my heart in a mess. I had a deep fear that my sacred space, my heart, would again be suddenly violated. Some part of me began protecting my heart by closing it and not trusting. Anyone.

By using EMDR therapy again, as well as placing all my attention on healing in any and every way I could find, I have been able to allow José into the innermost place in my heart. I have had visions of me standing before him, scared shitless that I will be hurt, scared as if I will die if he hurts me, and yet instead of closing up like the protective part of me wants to do, I choose to stay open. I stand with my chest and heart open to him, with my hands by my side. Sometimes in this vision I scream because I want to move my hands to my chest and say "NO" and close up, but I practice being open. I painstakingly practice and say "YES." Trusting. Having faith and letting him in. Again and again. I have become the most vulnerable I have ever been in my life, in a good, solid, loving relationship. The best relationship I have ever had.

My fears about becoming like those other women I read about, who could not be in a healthy relationship or have a healthy sex life, have totally dissolved. I am living proof that trauma, emotional, physical and even sexual in nature, can be healed by facing the healing journey head on and by radically choosing love – moment by moment.

Chapter 22

Dr. Ashanna Sevin

It has been over three years since the rape. I have completed my doctorate degree and now serve my community as a holistic chiropractor and healer. José and I have moved in together. We are deeply in love and committed to each other's highest good. He is such a devoted, loving partner, I could not ask for more. I have a wonderful community of friends in my life who continually inspire me to live more authentically from my heart. And I have found my voice, both by writing this book and sharing my story with groups to inspire them to be proactive in their healing.

I wish I could write, "And she lived happily ever after," but things are still very hard sometimes. I still have symptoms from the Cerebral Cysticercosis. And layers of PTSD from the assault keep appearing, even after I think that I am finished with it. There have been times when I see how much my healing process is affecting my partner, and when I see the pain in his face new layers of anger surface towards the man who raped me. I am no longer angry for the pain he caused me, but now I feel rage for the pain he is causing my beloved. But as my therapist recently told me, as she looked me squarely in the eyes, "You have done this before, you can do it again." And so my beautiful spiral continues as I revisit old wounds that need to be healed in different ways as time goes on. But each turn of the spiral things become easier, clearer, lighter. One foot in front of the other as I continue to choose compassion and service. And I continue to choose love for myself, my beloved, my friends and for you.

Epilogue

When I finished writing this book it was time to edit it. I began to go through it again and again, but before long my eyes were swirling with my own words. I no longer had perspective and felt like I needed help. I did not feel that I could ask anyone in particular to help me with my book, a huge project and favor to ask, so I meekly put a post on Facebook to inquire if anyone wanted to help. My story was so sacred to me I did not want just any ole' person, paid or not, to have their hand in directing how I delivered my heart's message, so I planned to have one, or at most only a few people copyedit it. I was surprised who responded; people I never would have guessed. My dad offered to proofread it, and many old friends came out of the woodwork offering to help. But something inside me was tugging at my sleeves. "Ask Elisha if she will edit the book for you. Ask Elisha, ask Elisha."

Elisha Norrie was the woman that I rented an apartment from in that gorgeous little town in New Zealand several years ago. The first part of my life story was written in the loving safety of her home. At that point I thought that my writing was part of my cleansing process, not something that I would necessarily publish. At that time, I knew of Elisha's history as a homeopath and counselor, and she became a source of amazing guidance for me when I lived in her home, and I considered her one of the teachers along my path. Yet I had not kept in good touch with her since I had left, even though I held her so dear to my heart.

Then one day I surrendered to that voice inside of me and I wrote her, out of the blue, to tell her I had written my memoir and needed help with it. Would she edit it? I kept feeling my intuition tell me to ask her, and I knew it was a huge project, but would she consider it?

I did not get a reply for many days and I felt I had overstepped my boundaries with her, asked too much and put her on the spot in an awkward way. I started to feel a little embarrassed that I had even asked.

Until I got her message. She wrote that since I had left New Zealand she had returned to university and now had a Master's Degree in Linguistics, and had continued with further postgraduate studies in writing and editing – and was now considering Ph.D. research in how writing memoirs can help people heal from trauma. Her previous years as a therapist showed her that a person's ability to open up and tell their story is a powerful tool in their healing process, also in line with current theories she was studying. Now that she was retired from practice, she wanted to further explore her own and others' memoir writing as a tool for personal development. But she was unsure if she wanted to commit to more study at this stage of her life, and was quietly waiting for a sign.

And then my email appeared. She got her sign – and I got the most synchronistic, mind-blowing email from her saying, emphatically, "Yes!" And not only yes, but she also shared the story of her studies and interests that I had not heard of until that moment.

I could not believe my eyes as I read this. It is one of those moments when I scratch my head and think that this is a little too magical for things to be just coincidence, one of those moments that makes you believe there has to be some master plan or spirit at work. So immediately I told my Facebook friends that I no longer needed their help, but thank you, and I sent the manuscript to Elisha.

I see now that I would not have been able to trust another editor like I trust her. I would not have been able to let someone else rework it, weaving things back in that I had taken out. She also asked me to write about other things in detail to fill in the gaps, restructuring it so it flows in a much better way to show you my journey, my innermost feelings.

I feel that Elisha and I are of like mind and heart, so I trusted her in this process. I started writing this book while I lived in her home, and now it has become what it is, with the aid of her hand and heart, based once more in her home in New Zealand. Part of the spiral, a beautiful example of how things circle back to where they began, yet on a higher level – more refined and conscious.

During our editing process together, old issues began to surface for me that needed further healing: symptoms from the Cerebral Cysticercosis and PTSD from the assault. When I first contacted Elisha I had stabilized at what I thought was a sustainably joyful place, thinking I was done with the bulk of my healing, especially from the rape. But new layers began to appear, layers that needed attention, layers that needed healing.

And thus, my editor also became my healer and health advisor. The one who was helping me comb through my past, my story, helping me craft it into something to be of service to others and give meaning to the madness I had lived, was also helping me gain perspective on what was happening to me now and gave me strength to keep going. She was able to identify where I was in my recovery, and that it was important to re-activate my network of therapists so that I could continue to have access to help if and when I might need it.

She also gave me permission to step into the role of a healer for others, my life's purpose, even though I doubted myself. I felt as though I didn't have everything figured out or healed on my end (who does though, really?) and therefore wasn't worthy or capable of being a healer for others. Elisha was able to share with me aspects of her own journey living with the effects of illness and trauma, herself a living example of how we can turn our suffering into wisdom and service. With her help I began to understand the concept of the "wounded healer," and that my past illness and trauma, along with my commitment to the ongoing healing process, were actually advantageous to my ability to be a good healer. She helped me to believe that I am a beautiful work in progress, and that I *am* a very effective facilitator to help others heal.

I have also come full circle to the message I wrote Reggie Leonard Jones, and I have needed to apply those very words to myself. I saw a vision for him, which despite the challenges he faces in life, he still has the power to choose love.

I truly believe that he has that choice: he can choose love. And so can I.

It is so incredibly easy for me to fall into a victim role and want to close my heart. But if I truly meant what I wrote to him, that I am someone who chooses love, then I have to be aligned with my words.

I have to live love.

To put love into action, the greatest power for change.

In this we are similar.

I can choose those beautiful visions of service for myself – and live life with love.

But I am the one who has to choose.

I have to choose.

And I do.

Epi-epilogue

I am not sure if there is such a thing as an epi-epilogue, but here it is. Leave it to me to make up a crazy new thing… I began writing this book in 2010. It is now 2023. In the years since its publication, I was married and divorced, I raised my two step-children for 12 years, I healed from yet another bout of parasites that made me incredibly ill, had a total hip replacement, created and run a nonprofit, and cultivated a private practice offering chiropractic care, functional medicine and other mind-body healing resources and classes in the Bay Area. I have experienced some major healing in this last year, and I will try my best to convey these experiences to you.

In 1999, when I had the grand mal seizure, I had the experience of dying. I experienced myself as a singular point of consciousness in an infinite field of white/prismatic energy. Since I thought I was dying, I thought I would stay in that place forever, but that "field" told me, "You are not finished yet. You have some work to do". And I was sent back into my body, and a little bit later woke from the seizure. It turns out that during that extremely long and intense seizure, I torqued my hips so badly that I needed a total hip replacement at the age of 45, and I dislocated my shoulder causing dysfunctional movement and pain for years, which has recently flared due to the stress of my divorce. This experience also launched me into many years of scary and challenging experiences of healing from the brain tumors that caused the periods of blindness and the seizures.

Now, in 2023, I recently went to a meditation retreat and had the most profound experience. In a huge room full of 1800 people, I learned about the science of meditation and the anatomy of the body in depth to be able to practice moving cerebral spinal fluid up to the brain to activate the pineal gland. I had studied yoga, breathwork, and meditation for decades but had never experienced such powerful meditations as I did at that retreat. It was as if all the things I had studied and been interested in during my life coalesced into a coherent practice and I feel so grateful that I received those teachings.

After one of these meditations, we were on a break. Everyone started talking to one another and moving about to go to the restroom or get a snack. I turned to the person on my left and all of a sudden a shock of energy struck me like a lightning bolt, and although no time at all passed in that room, I had a huge experience of going back to that moment of the seizure. Quite unexpectedly. Except for this time, instead of being that singular point of consciousness, I was the entire field. And I told myself (my past self), "You are not finished. You have some work to do", and then all of a sudden I was back in the room at the retreat. It was as if in that moment, I was the point of consciousness, AND I was the field, and I experienced the vibration of everything, all at once, everywhere. It was difficult for me to talk about, as you can imagine, but it was such an incredible experience of completing some sort of loop, a deep healing of that moment so long ago, folding my life into no-time. The 24 years in between disappearing but also the journey through life necessary to bring me to that point.

At the retreat, I asked to be a healee to heal my shoulder, as it still pained me, and I am a chiropractor so it was making my work challenging on a physical level. Despite practicing yoga and healing dance, and seeing a myriad of doctors and healers for my shoulder it seemed that it was not healing. And I was chosen to receive that healing at the retreat, which included 2400 people channeling healing energy into my body/field/me. However, my experience of healing my shoulder became SO MUCH MORE that the physical pain, in ways I never would have expected.

In one of these healings, I experienced a powerful moment of healing myself so fully, feeling all the parts of myself from the time I was a baby to the moment of my death. I could feel the essence of healing inside of all people in the world, at all times, all at once. Every cell, every atom, all of the energy of everyone, everything, and everywhere. It was truly a moment of enlightenment (or so it seemed to me in my limited experience). And it all happened in a sober moment of meditation, with the added energy of so many people. It was by far the most exquisite and beautiful moment of my life. It was truly a quantum healing.

But it has been challenging to integrate this profound experience back in the real world. I returned home to filling out divorce paperwork, spending hours at the DMV, dealing with a bashed in window from my car. I am in inquiry right now about how to find the beauty and joy in these moments of real life when I must do things that I truly do not seem to enjoy. It is a constant and challenging practice to keep that coherent feeling of gratitude when I don't feel so grateful for the things I feel I have to do that I don't want to do.

Lately, with a fresh start, I find myself praying and meditating on envisioning my dream life, and doing the massive amount of work that it takes to get there. It reminds me of doing this same thing back in the Namib desert when I was a Peace Corps Volunteer. And I radically dedicated my life to realizing that calling of being a healer. It has been both my joy and spiritual practice to serve my community as a doctor of chiropractic and functional medicine specialist, a Reiki and meditation teacher, and a rehabilitation therapist. Now, I am in the process of uplevelling my life in all the ways that I can. And I encourage all of my patients to do the same. I encourage YOU to do the same. We are all on this path together. I want everyone to live their dream life. We all deserve to do that. And more than likely, anyone reading this book has the privilege of realizing those dreams through setting intentions, aligning their energy and life to manifest/create that. The road is not easy, but it is so deeply fruitful and fulfilling, at least to me.

Bless you all for being on the journey with me. I deeply bow to all of you and love that you are reading this book. I hope you may be inspired by my own walk of tribulation, growth, periods of joy and learning. May it be of service to you and the world. And so it is.

247

Acknowledgements

This book has taken a long time to write, and it started and came to completion with my friend Elisha Norrie in orbit. As an editor, she helped bring *A Beautiful Spiral* to life, and as a counselor, she has been a tremendous source of guidance for my healing. I am forever grateful for this incredible woman being in my life in all the many facets that she is.

I owe thanks to all the doctors, therapists and healers that have helped me along the way; there are too many to count. They not only helped me heal myself, but taught me how to be a healer as well.

I am grateful for the United States Peace Corps. This organization does amazing work in the world, and I loved serving in Namibia as a volunteer. I count it as a very precious time in my life. Even though I contracted the Cerebral Cysticercosis during my service, I view it as an essential part of my path.

The local government contacted me after the assault happened and asked what they could do for me. I asked them to honor the detectives that worked on my case. Those men are the kind of men you want working for the police; strong, good-hearted men who work hard and truly care. Somehow they are hard as nails and yet soft and tender at the right times. Sean, Ray, Rick and all the others, I thank you for your support and your work.

I am in awe of the wonderful friends in my life, Sweet Snugs and beyond. You continue to teach me how to transform challenges into love, how to live with integrity, how to weave dance into my days, and I cannot imagine life without you, my community. Thank you.

My family has been a constant source of love, support and learning. We are a bunch of good people who accept the differences in one another and love each other no matter what. For that I am ever impressed and appreciative.

I especially thank my brother, Travis, for being one of my greatest teachers in life, and for coming to my aid so many times, especially when I needed help getting my life back together after the assault.

Lastly, I want to thank myself. I know that may seem strange, but although I still have so much to learn, I know in my bones that I have given every ounce of my energy to healing, co-creating (with Spirit) the life of my dreams, and being of service. I am proud of myself for doing the work. It's hard. But I have reached down deep inside myself to find strength during times when I have wanted to cave in and give up. I have "adulted" when all I want is to chill out or even run away. It has always paid off in the biggest ways. And I am living that life that I have set my compass needle to. I live in so much gratitude.

Printed in Great Britain
by Amazon

45847047R00148